MW01028181

MASTER
OF THE WAITING ROOM

The Professional Service
Advisor Sales Approach

by Steven E. Shaw

Master of the Waiting Room
The Professional Service Advisor Sales Approach
Copyright © 2016

For permission requests, write to the publisher, addressed "Attention: Permissions Coordinator," at the address below.

Steven E. Shaw

steve@steveshawtraining.com

Printed in U.S.A

TABLE OF CONTENTS

Part One - The Sales Approach

Part Two - Transition to Real World Selling

(Intentionally Left Blank)

A Word For My Friends and New Relations

This book is dedicated to all of the professional men and women in the automotive industry that I have known and who I call my friend. There is a list longer than the book itself of the many who have shaped my mind and my outlook. If we have crossed paths and said more than a hello, I have breathed in your spirit, somehow taken the best of it and made it a part of my being. I trust you smile knowing that you have influenced my life.

To the most personal of you who I call regularly for love and advice, Bob Cawley, James Gross, John Kerley, Ron Kiepke, Bob Palcher, Terry Chechakli, Paul Webb, Jeff Zwerling, Gregg Thornton, Rick Strifler, Jeff Pister, Hal Makorow, Corey Smith, Janet Hayworth, Joe DeLuigi, Frank Parra, John Schnepp, Ken Kocher, Nick Sansone, Yegor Malinovskii, Rob Sneed along with my entire rolodex of daily contacts I say with deepest sincerity that I appreciate the friendship and our bond. You all inspire me to be a better professional and a good servant.

I travel everyday to bring each service advisor a better paycheck and peace in your job. I travel everyday to make up crazy ideas for management to help improve your process. I travel everyday because I want you to generate more sales and gross profit. I travel everyday because I am passionate about your triumph. Mostly, I travel everyday because I can think of nothing better than to have you share your wisdom with me. I am one lucky man!

This book is a culmination of my passion, my drive and desire for our shared success!

To everyone I salute!

Steve Shaw

Part 1

The Sales Approach

(Intentionally Left Blank)

Master of the Waiting Room - The Professional Service Advisor Sales Approach

INTRODUCTION

John Schnepp
Crown Automotive Group
Pinellas County Service Director

Every craftsman knows the value of the right tool in the right hands. In this book, Steve has assembled a collection of tools worthy of the most expert of service advisors and accompanied them with step-by-step instructions for their implementation. The pages that follow represent years of experience and are a culmination of tried and true methods that yields proven results.

In the five years that Steve has been training advisors in our dealer group, we have enjoyed improvement in sales, gross profit along with many key performance indicators such as customer pay hours per repair order and dollars per repair order. We have also seen improvements in our CSI scores and customer retention.

Steve's unique presentation style engages the audience at every level. This skill has not been neglected in the chapters you are about to read. This book will put your career as a service advisor on the fast track and put you and those you care about on the path to realizing your financial goals. It is an investment that will pay dividends long after the pages have begun to yellow. Enjoy the journey on which you are embarking. Enjoy becoming the ***Master of YOUR Waiting Room.***

The Value Proposition

The value proposition simply states that the perceived value of an item must exceed the cost of that same item. Customers want to feel as if they are getting a great deal for their dollar. The more "VALUE" that is provided to an item for sale, the more money a consumer is willing to spend on that said item. The value is assigned to an object based upon the actual desires of a customer. If a customer perceives that there is no particular need for an item, the cost, no matter how low the price, becomes insignificant to the purchase. The consumer does not buy. The reverse says based on a high need and high value, no matter how high the cost, the consumer is willing to make a purchase. Customers are willing to make a purchase at the market rate, and sometimes higher, based on their view of the value assigned to the item.

In recent years customers left the dealerships because they did not see the value in dealership service. The Internet has allowed the customer to shop for the best price without leaving their homes. This led many dealerships to become very cost conscious instead of becoming value conscious. Dealership Service lost a competitive edge in the marketplace due to the perception that the dealership was not the only shop to competently repair or service a new car. The independent shop stole the work that was once only performed at the dealership. The dealership in most cases is a better, higher quality option for the consumer based on many factors, yet through marketing the independent world captured a once-captive market.

Now is the time to change that picture. The challenge for dealership service departments (and most importantly, dealership service advisors who rely on customer pay service income to earn a living) to return the perception of the quality of dealer service on its head and SELL the customer on the idea that the dealership is the best place for auto service.

This book is dedicated to the professional service advisor: the professional service advisor who is dedicated to his/her customer. It's time to make real money on the service drive and create that coveted customer retention that everyone is ranting about these days.

*It is time to bring back VALUE to the dealership.
The dealership is worth it. The service and the service
advisor is worth it.
It is time to get paid for the work that we do!*

It is now time to become the

1 Why Customers Buy

Why customers say no

Customers drive into the service department with the hopes of meeting a service consultant or consumer advocate. They are looking for someone, anyone, who can help them through the process of the repair. They are hoping to find an advisor, someone who relates to them to ensure a smooth transition back to the normal driving condition. Their typical visit to the shop finds a customer in the presence of a person who wants to be an advocate, yet presents themselves as salespeople.

The presence of a salesperson hikes up the level of stress in the customer, and as a result, service advisors all too often find them bombarded with every imaginable objection to having the work done. These objections range from the mundane budget protest to using the excuse of lack of time, calling for a second opinion, and even to absurd name-calling, such as "rip off artist" as depicted by local fare...

Objections overheard on the service drive are:

- ✓ I do not have any money
- ✓ I have to get somewhere
- ✓ I have waited too long;
- ✓ You cost too much money,
- ✓ That's too expensive
- ✓ I can do it myself,
- ✓ I only deal with men/women,
- ✓ I have my own mechanic,
- ✓ Do you offer coupons?
- ✓ (and my personal favorite): can I get a discount?

The service advisor is put into a defensive posture and often forced to retreat to feeling guilty for simply pointing out the nature of the customer's problem. Once into retreat, the chances of recovery diminish greatly. This leads to lower key performance indicators such as dollars per RO, Hours Per RO, declining ELR and naturally disgruntled technicians in the shop.

Understanding key elements in the customers' psyches can eliminate this defensive posture, improve RO performance, advance positive morale and skyrocket paychecks. It is vital for a service advisor to be aware of the real desires of the customer. Service advisors are sometimes led astray by thinking that the customer came in to have good service, or that the customer somehow showed up at the dealership because we are nice people. Many service advisors fall for the notion that the customer wants their vehicle fixed at a cheap price. The biggest trap that the service advisor falls into is that the customer has no money for their repairs. The real issue is that customers have underlying desires that the service advisor must fulfill if there is to be a sale.

The Four Desires of the Customer

Customers choose to have their vehicle repaired or serviced for one or more of these four primary desires: 1) Safety, 2) Reliability - Dependability, 3) Performance and 4) Protecting their Investment. These four desires are the ONLY requirements of the customer coming to the shop.

SAFETY - Moms, Dads, Grandparents, Aunts and Uncles alike are traveling the roads of cities and towns. They care solely that the occupants of the vehicle are strapped in and arrive safely at their destination. Driving on the road today is dangerous. At any moment, road hazards can pop up and turn a nice drive, a vacation or a routine trip to the office into a deadly situation. These same customers of service spent a great deal of time selecting their current vehicle based on the brand standards of safety. Customers pay a large portion of their resources to ensure that their basic safety needs are satisfied.

RELIABILITY / DEPENDABILITY - It is important that the car starts and runs every day. People rely on their vehicles to get from point A to Z each day. Some people need their cars for work or for school. Others simply use their car as transport to the train station or airport. Only with proper reliable transportation can the task be completed. Every buyer needs the peace of mind that the vehicle is going to operate each time as needed.

I have been using Steve Shaw's techniques for 4 years now, and I continue to see my sales increase month after month. Steve's techniques are not only applicable in the work place; one can apply these techniques to the routine of everyday life."

Corey Smith – Toyota Service Advisor

PERFORMANCE - Customers want a certain level of performance from their vehicles. This performance can mean different things to different customers - for some, it may be the speed of their Mustang GT or Dodge Challenger, such astaking the turns at high speeds hugging the curves. On the other hand, performance can be as simple as being comfortable in the Lincoln Navigator. Performance is also represented by the style of the car or the image of the brand. . If I am a customer, this image represents an extension of myself, and my ego is dependent on the vehicle's performance.

PROTECTING THE INVESTMENT - A vehicle is often the number one investment in a consumer's life. If the customer owns a home, then their vehicle is the number two investment of a lifetime. Most people want to protect their investments. Protecting the investment is important in two ways. The first is for the customer who plans on keeping their car for a long time. Some customers keep their vehicle for 100,000 - 200,000 miles. Other customers are interested in trading in their vehicle every year or so. In either case, the customer wants to protect this major investment. However, the customer also wants to save money on their vehicle repairs and wants to ensure the most value for their dollar.

These four desires, safety, reliability, performance and protecting their investment are the sole reasons for customer contact with the service department of the dealership. Customers are not coming in to the dealership because the service advisor is nice. They are not coming into the dealership because the service advisor has a friendly attitude. Customers are not driving in to see the service advisor and spending a sizeable amount of money for any other reason than they need their vehicle to be safe, to start every day, to maintain a level of performance, or to save them money in the future. Period!

It is fair to say that the customer who is stranded on the side of the road does not care who or what service advisor helps them at that moment of need. Imagine being stranded with a disabled vehicle. The most important thing is to get to safety, and next is to get back to normal. Most people will pay whatever it takes to get back to normal. The college student, parent or worker needs their transportation to ensure they complete a class, graduate or simply pay the bills. Accepting this perspective makes the service advisor able to relate to the consumer and provide the necessary approach to servicing the vehicle.

Additionally, Often a customer will purchase the loss leader special vehicle in the newspaper or on the Internet. Customers flock to the store for a chance at a cheap vehicle. Many times that same buyer who could not be bothered with extended warranties, gap or other finance items sign their paperwork and head directly to the performance shop. They open their pocket book for rims, spoilers, performance items and accessories. The dealership was trying to sell items and the customer wanted performance. The customer wanted to look cool or go fast. Finally, the ability to save money on repairs is important in the aspect of protecting the investment. This is a key component to customer sales and retention.

Customer Retention dictates that it is important to be nice. The soft skills and experience are necessary to keep the customer returning to the dealership for service, and most importantly, returning to the trusted service advisor. The best way is to be nice and provide the experience that the customer enjoys, while serving the real desires that make the customer willing to purchase service from you.

Needs and Wants

It is important to distinguish between "needs" and "wants". The best way to keep things simple is to say that customer needs are those items that are required and that have serious consequences if they are not completed. On the other hand, wants are desires that a customer would like to have, yet there are no significant consequences if they are not completed. Examples of needs for the customer are items including: brakes, battery, tires, fluid services, and alignments. In fact, every item on the Multi-Point Inspection (MPI) form are needed items. Examples of wants are items such as a remote starter, spoilers, accessories and even a detail service. There is no consequence to the customer if these "wants" are not completed on the vehicle. Based upon this discussion even a simple oil change is a NEED that must be completed or the manufacturer's warranty could be compromised. Each one of the customer's desires:safety, performance, reliability and investment protection can be compromised (consequences) if the items from the MPI are not performed. This makes it a fact that all the items on the multi-point inspection are REQUIRED in order to ensure safety, reliability/dependability, protect their investment or to maintain a high level of performance. The service advisor can present any item from the MPI as a requirement to maintain one of the four desires of the customer.

Features and Benefits

From day one in the dealership managers discuss selling, most importantly, the features and benefits of a product or service. Trainers from all walks of industry have slightly different ideas on how to educate sales persons. In this discussion the focus is to make selling easy for service advisors. The easiest way to describe a feature is to say that it is *any product or service offered by the dealership*. The best way to describe a benefit is to say that it is *the specific advantage to the customer*. Some say *"What's in it for me? (WIFM)."*

Power steering is a <u>feature</u> on a new car. The <u>benefit</u> to power steering is easier turning control of the vehicle or better *performance* of the vehicle. Another feature of a new car could be a *BOSE sound system*. The benefit to the customer is high quality sound or better performance of the radio.

Feature = Power Steering	*Feature = Bose Sound System*
Benefit = Performance	*Benefit = Performance*

Another way to look at this difference from the service perspective is the example of the water pump. The water pump is a feature that is offered in the service department. The water pump *(feature)* simply circulates coolant around the engine. The **benefit** is that by having this water circulating, the engine stays at optimal operating temperature, which prevents premature wear *(protects investment)* prevents breakdowns, *(safety* and *reliability)* and maximizes efficiency *(performance)*.

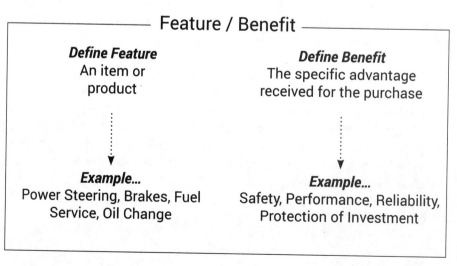

— Feature / Benefit —

Define Feature
An item or product

Define Benefit
The specific advantage received for the purchase

Example...
Power Steering, Brakes, Fuel Service, Oil Change

Example...
Safety, Performance, Reliability, Protection of Investment

Feature or Benefit Exercise

Are the items below a feature or benefit? Check the correct answer for the items below.

MPI	☐ Feature	☐ Benefit
Water Pump	☐ Feature	☐ Benefit
Goodyear Belt	☐ Feature	☐ Benefit
Tires	☐ Feature	☐ Benefit
Road Hazard Wrty	☐ Feature	☐ Benefit
Run Flat Tires	☐ Feature	☐ Benefit
12/12 Warranty	☐ Feature	☐ Benefit
OEM Parts	☐ Feature	☐ Benefit
Factory Trained Techs	☐ Feature	☐ Benefit
Power Steering Hose	☐ Feature	☐ Benefit
Dealership	☐ Feature	☐ Benefit
Dealership Oil Change	☐ Feature	☐ Benefit
You (Service Advisor)	☐ Feature	☐ Benefit

As one reads this exercise the items may appear to be both a feature and a benefit. This is the confusing part. Many service advisors actually confuse the feature with the benefit. Or sometimes service advisors actually present the feature as if it is a benefit.

Contemplate this: is a Multi-Point Inspection a feature or a benefit? Many initially believe the MPI is a benefit. Sounds right? Actually a MPI is a feature that dealerships offer their customers. Correct? The benefit to the customer of having an MPI completed is that it provides the benefit of knowing the vehicle is safe, reliable, and performing well, thus preserving the value of the vehicle.

Imagine a customer waking up in the morning. Do you think they wake up and say, "Gee, I really like Bob at the dealership; maybe I'll go spend $800 on a water pump"?

Or

Would the customer more likely say, "I need to keep my family safe, Ill go spend $800 on a water pump".

It is always about safety, performance, reliability and protecting the investment.

#1 Features and Benefits of the Dealership - With Value Statement

It is important for every service advisor to have knowledge of all of the dealership features. Dealer Principals spend an enormous amount of money providing their customers the finest amenities, items and people. Dealerships provide features such as factory trained technicians to provide the highest quality, which protects their investment, additional features of the dealership are...

Feature:		Benefit:
✔ Expertise of Sales and Service Personnel	to	Protect Investment
✔ Factory Parts (OEM Parts)	to	Give Best Performance
✔ Comfortable Waiting Rooms	to	Provide Comfort (Performance)
✔ Extended Hours	to	Provide Convenience
✔ Shuttles	to	Provide Convenience
✔ Alternative Transportation	to	Provide Convenience
✔ Competitive, Pre-Discounted Prices (Save Money)	to	Protect the Customer's Investment
✔ DMS, History Capture (Save Money)	to	Protect the Customer's Investment
✔ Extended Hours	to	Provide Convenience

The list can go on and on. The vital part of knowing this is to be able to share it with the customers. Research shows that convenience is the number one reason a customer may defect to another facility. The customer needs to know what the dealership provides. This builds value!

By knowing all of the features and benefits of the dealership, service advisors can create their VALUE STATEMENT. This value statement comes into play when selling and overcoming objections.

A value statement may sound like this...

At our dealership we provide our customers with the highest quality services at the best possible prices. In fact, we shop the market regularly to ensure we are competitive. We offer our customers...

Factory Trained Technicians to keep your vehicle safe...Our technicians train over 80 hours per year to know your vehicle better than anyone. This ensures the highest performance of your vehicle...We are the only shop in this market that represents exclusive Factory Parts to protect your investment...Our Dealership Management System tracks and monitors your services and history to ensure that we take care of your vehicle to your standards and save you money throughout your ownership experience...We have pre-discounted menu prices to ensure you get the best possible price on repairs as well.

As the tools unfold in the book this value statement becomes more and more important. This is especially true in overcoming customer objections.

Features and Benefits of You - the Service Advisor - With a Personal Value Statement

Now it is as important or maybe even more important for the customer to understand us - the service advisors. Imagine how to answer when a customer asks why should they should service their car with you. It is vital to have identified one's own features and benefits. For instance, some advisors could say :

Feature:		Benefit:
✓ A Factory Trained Service Advisor	to	Protect Your Investment (Save Money)
✓ 15 Years Experience	to	keep you Safe
✓ College Educated	to	understand your needs
✓ Single Parent	to	aware of the need to save you money
✓ New to the business	to	provide a fresh perspective, provide convenience
✓ New to Service Writing	to	Get things done - Convenience

Customers often ask service advisors in many (sometimes indirect) ways why they should service their cars with us. For example, some customer comments are:

✓ I have my own mechanic

✓ I would like a second opinion

This is telling service advisors that the customer is not sold on our opinion or explanation. Many times the customer needs reassurance that the service advisor is the expert. Simply having a prepared value statement about you can help overcome this reluctance. A personal value statement may sound similar to this...

> I am an expert service advisor with 15 years of experience working on this brand
>
> of vehicles. My job is to guide you through the ownership experience and protect
>
> your investment. I do this with a combination of factory training, college experience,
>
> and husband (or wife) skills. It is my duty to make sure your vehicle performs to
>
> your standards, including ensuring your safety and reliability and protecting your
>
> investment over the life of the vehicle.

2 Presenting Multi-Point Inspections

The Multi-Point Inspection

The Multi-Point Inspection (MPI) is probably the most important tool in the service advisor arsenal. This MPI if done correctly can provide the service advisor thousands of additional dollars in added business and in personal pay. This same MPI can also be devastating to the service advisor if done poorly. Over the years the MPI has evolved dramatically.

Evolution of MPI

The evolution of the MPI is interesting to relive and understand. The MPI stems from a customer pay maintenance culture. Import franchises such as Toyota and Honda have traditionally developed a maintenance culture where customers are groomed to maintain their cars. Domestic franchises like GM, Ford and Chrysler conventionally had a warranty culture. Customers looked upon oil changes as a necessary evil, and maintenance was a second thought and rarely performed at the dealership. It is important to learn and be aware of the MPI evolution.

The MPI or vehicle inspection began to get traction in the late 1990s as dealerships began to understand the importance of customer pay business. Throughout car dealer history, the technician would look over the customer's vehicle in hopes of finding additional work. Most technicians and dealers called this an UPSELL Circa 1997, Ford Motor Company launched an initiative called "Around the Wheel". This started a revolution in the auto dealership industry. Ford Motor Company representatives taught the Ford Dealer that a proper vehicle inspection with a full-color report was the best way to ensure the customer would maintain their vehicle and spend coveted dollars at the dealership. This set the MPI revolution in motion.

This evolution was done to prepare the dealership that the warranty dollars were going away. That is exactly what happened. Vehicles began to have better quality, and the warranty money went away. Many dealerships embraced this new initiative and became successful in a new environment. Other dealerships scoffed at the thought of performing the dreaded oil change and resisted. These dealerships suffered, and there are many that still under-perform in customer pay business. In the Ford world, dealerships used the operation code 99P and added a separate line on the RO to indicate to the technician that a Multi-Point Inspection was to be performed. It may be hard to comprehend that to this day as this book is being read, some dealership still do not have a functional MPI process at their store. The dealerships that still resist are struggling due to the lack of customer-pay dollars, and they must rely on slimmer warranty monies. As soon as the industry adopted this new approach to customer pay business, most manufacturers created their own MPI forms for the dealership.

Many service advisors believe that because the car came into the service department, the customer naturally wanted an inspection. In fact, some service advisors still sneak an MPI line on the RO without asking for permission, as if this technique is going to work on the customer. It may be harsh to hear that customers resent sneaky techniques. Customers want a transparent transaction. Customers want to be asked their permission to perform any repairs or services on their vehicle.

Quarter Time

One can argue who actually coined the term or process known as Quarter-Time; however, this next step in the process moved customer pay business forward dramatically.

> Quarter-Time is a term for the time that is required to complete the Multi-Point Inspection and present the results to the customer. This means, for example, an Oil Change and Tire Rotation must be completed in 60 Minutes (or less hopefully). The MPI must be presented in ¼ of the Total Service Time or 15 minutes of the RO being printed. This 15 minutes is known as Quarter Time.

Dealerships who have adopted this service philosophy have seen dramatic improvements in Customer Pay Performance. Many dealership managers and principals think they have a quality MPI Quarter Time Process, yet they do not really have one. Without a fully functional Quarter Time Process the dealership is stuck at average RO performance and mostly negative perceptions of an express lane. This means that the dealerships without

Quarter Time will perform fast oil changes at a loss and never fully recognize the profit center that quick oil changes can yield. A fully functional process will deliver tremendous results. Service Advisors that want to sell more service immediately without any changes to their selling approach can implement a Quarter Time Process. Most customers are willing to spend additional monies on their vehicle if it will be completed quickly in the allotted amount of time. Even with a complete set of power tools and techniques that will be in the following paragraphs, sales performance will remain poor without Quarter Time.

Here is a documented process that works: **Quarter Time Process**

ASM		▸ Meets customer on service drive, identifies the 45 minute process ▸ Reviews history in the Manufacturer Dealer Service Advisor Portal ▸ Presents necessary maintenance needs based on time and mileage ▸ Writes pre-write (or RO) ▸ Turns on flashers in service drive ▸ 45-Minute Service Begins
Porter	5:00	▸ Immediately drives vehicle to Fast Lane in shop
Tech	10:00	▸ Reviews Pre-Write and determines best course of action - Works with dispatch to log in RO ▸ Performs services as described on RO (Works Oil Change) ▸ Begins MPI reviewing under hood items
	25:00	▸ Completes MPI and walks to ASM ▸ Completes the work as described on RO
	35:00	▸ Hands completed RO to Service Advisor ▸ Parks vehicle on service drive ▸ Walks back to staging area for next RO
ASM	40:00	▸ Completes paperwork (bills and books RO) ▸ Prints invoice in ASM office
ASM	45:00	▸ Greets customer and cashiers invoice ▸ Clock stops on oil change ▸ Customer departs and is happy

MPI Evolution, Continued

As dealerships developed fast lanes and Quarter time processes, the MPI has continued to evolve. In the beginning, the service forms were simple color-coded Red, Yellow, and Green to signify the condition of the vehicle components. Service advisors were taught to talk to the customer about the GREEN items first. This was a great theory back then. The reasoning was to tell the customer about the green items because we do not want to hit the customer over the head with the bad stuff first. Now some people say, "sell the green". Ok...Whatever! The customer is not buying this sales tactic. There must be a better way...

Many service advisors confuse the quote with the MPI. It is of the highest importance that service advisors distinguish between these two tools. The MPI is the inspection and complementary form that is reviewed with the customer. The quote is the price list to complete any additional services that are required.

This quote presentation process has evolved over time as well.

The Grand Total Approach

In the late 1980s and early 1990s, service advisors were instructed to create a list of all required services and repairs and create a grand total for the customer. Service advisors were to give the customer one price for everything and say, "The total cost today is $954. I can have this all completed while you wait or by the end of the day. Would you like to take care of this all today?" This is selling the Grand Total.

The RIM Method

As customer pay work evolved and the economy changed, the presentation style changed as well. An approach called RIM was developed as a way to present the estimate to the customer. Many still use this approach today. It is an effective way to prioritize the services for the customer. This is how RIM works.

RIM stands for...

R = Items **_Related_** to the Primary Concern

I = Items that need **_Immediate_** attention

M = **_Maintenance_** Items that are due

This approach is best used when service advisors feel that categorizing the items for the customer is best. In this situation, the service advisor presents the prime item to the customer. Once the primary concern is sold, the service advisor presents related items. For instance, if a customer had a "service engine soon" light on, and the proper repair is to replace an oxygen sensor, one could consider a fuel service or spark plugs as related to the prime item. The service advisor would summarize the total price of each category and present three smaller totals instead of the grand total.

The immediate needs could be brake pads, as they are worn down to 2mm. The maintenance requirements could be a coolant service or possibly the next scheduled maintenance service due.

This is the RIM selling method.

Line by Line

As the economy turned, many service advisors shifted away from the grand total and the RIM method and simply presented items individually. Service Advisors would make a list of the technician's inspection items and organize it in order of importance. Many felt it was just easier to sell one or two of the most important items. This method requires the service advisor to give the customer an itemized or line-by-line total of the needs of the vehicle. Often this is simply written on the back of the RO.

This is the line-by-line selling method.

Steve Shaw Training approach taught me how to improve my performance by sharing the value to my customers. Steve's in depth method to explaining the vehicle health report allowed me to explain the vehicle's maintenance needs to the customer in a way that they felt the importance of the service." **Grace Hardin** – Ford Service Advisor

Which method is Best?

All three methods work! Each service advisor has a different style. The question becomes, "Which one is the best?" The answer is "It depends on how the customer wants it". Service advisors can ask the customer how they like to be sold. (Revealed soon)

The No-Win Scenario

For anyone who is a Star Trek fan or geek, you may remember what is known as the no-win situation. It is called The Kobayashi Maru scenario. Here is what happened.

> According to MemoryAlpha.com, The **Kobayashi Maru scenario** was an infamous no-win scenario that was part of the curriculum for command-track cadets at Starfleet Academy in the 23rd century. It was primarily used to assess a cadet's discipline, character and command capabilities when facing an impossible situation, as there is no (legitimate) strategy that will result in a successful outcome.

The Dealership No-Win Scenario - Or The Journey to the Waiting Room

As the service advisor approaches the waiting room, often angst blows across the customers. Heads turn as if a hated teacher was about to call on a forgetful student in class. The wisdom in the waiting room is "Do not come and see me". Customers squirm in their seats as the service advisor walks in to present additional "up sells". Nobody wins in this scenario. Other service advisors ask the customer to walk to a dedicated quiet spot. The rest of the waiting room sighs in relief because they were not called out. The wisecrack customer barks out…"do not buy anything; call my friend for a second opinion." Even better is when a service advisor pages on the intercom to have the customer report to the service drive. It is similar to getting called to the principal's office. The service advisor is in the NO WIN Situation.

The Typical MPI Presentation - Or Sales Pitch

Many service advisors use the follow word tracks to pitch a customer.

> Mr/Ms Customer, remember the MPI we talked about earlier. Everything looks good on your car, but my technician found some things wrong and has some recommendations for you."

This is one of the worst sales pitches one can throw out. As soon as this comes out of the service advisor's mouth, the customer builds walls then concocts as many objections as they can think of in the spur of the moment. The typical situation continues by the service advisor presenting a laundry list of recommendations. The customer's eyes glass over, the presentation accelerates and then deteriorates rapidly. The presentation often concludes with the customer saying, "Just wrap it up." Finally the service advisor replies, "It's your call; I just need to tell you." The sale is over and the prophecy is fulfilled. The customer has no money, the customer is a mooch, the customer is not buying today.

Like James Tiberius Kirk of the Starship Enterprise, it's time to change the conditions of the test. It is time to revise the most effective way to present the MPI to the customer. It is time to turn the tables in the waiting room. It is time to stop selling and turn the customer into a buyer. Now is the time to become the ***MASTER OF THE WAITING ROOM.***

The Approach to Master the Waiting Room

Ask For Permission to Perform the Multi-Point Inspection

The way to master the waiting room is to present items that require attention to the customer in a way where the customer perceives they are in control of the situation. It is important for the customer to feel they are driving this entire sales approach. The service advisor must ask the customer for permission to complete a complete health check on their vehicle. The best word tracks sound like this...

> We offer our customers a comprehensive health report (Multi-Point Inspection) on their vehicle. It is important that you know everything about your car when you leave here today. How does that sound?

The customer will want to know everything about their #1 or #2 Investment in life. Remember, the car is often an extension of their self. The will want to know if asked properly.

The next step is to complete the primary concern. The primary concern is what the customer drove into the store to have completed. It could be a simple oil change or a "check engine" light flashing on the instrument panel. Always ensure this is identified and completed before mentioning any additional items regarding the multi-point inspection.

Once this is complete, the service advisor can ask for permission to review the results of the multi-point inspection report.

> **Mr/Ms Customer, remember the health report we spoke about earlier, would this be a good time to review the results? I just need a few minutes of your time. Do you prefer to know all the details or would you like to hear the highlights?**

Once the Service Advisor has permission to review the results, the fun can begin. Permission has been granted, and the customer has blocked out the appropriate amount of time to hear the inspection results. This is how it's done.

Always start by educating the customer on how the report is viewed.

> **Customer Name**

It is VITAL to call the customer by their name. Their name can be either proper name as Mr / Ms or it can be just using their first name. Utilize the rapport level already established.

> **Year – Make – Model – Specific Mileage**

Many customers are unaware of the specifics on their vehicle. Typically polls find under 40% of customers know the exact details about their own vehicle. And to truly master the waiting room, it is key to advise all the other listeners in the waiting room of what is happening. Remember everyone is listening to the performance right now!

> **Mr Shaw, your 2013 Fiat 500 has 42,345 miles.**

The customer now knows more about their car than when they came in. The service advisor is obviously an expert on the vehicle. If by chance the customer does know the exact mileage, the service advisor just proved to the customer that they know as much as the customer and they are still the expert. The customer and the service advisor are seeing eye-to-eye.

Next and most importantly, most customers identify with their cars. In many cases the customer has a personal relationship with their car. The car is as important as some family members or more. The best way to capitalize on this relationship is to present the facts like their children's report card. When children pass a class, parents get excited. They take pictures, post on social media and tell their friends ad nauseam. They are naturally proud and pound their chest.

When a child fails a test, the parent is drawn to action. Some parents immediately hire a tutor, some ground their kids, some give more love. All take action. Action is what is wanted here with the MPI.

Many service advisors present the items "Green - Yellow - Red" because they do not want the customer to feel like they're hearing a sales presentation. Others simply say, "Sell the green". This is only confusing the customer. Customers have a false sense of security, and then the hammer comes down when the recommendations flow.

Start at the top of the MPI. The best verbiage is so simple.

> **Green Items - Pass our Vehicle Inspection**
> **Red Items - Fail our Vehicle Inspection**

Even if the first item is a fail, present it confidently. The customer, like the parent, will be drawn to action. The customer will engage and listen at attention. The customer's eyes will pop open and even their jaw will drop. This is a FACT about the car, just like a report card. Continue through the MPI line-by-line or group-by-group based on the specific manufacturer MPI report. Just like a visit to the doctor's office, money is never discussed in a health report. Present the facts as PASS or FAIL. Completely review each section or category.

Review the entire MPI Report from top to bottom left to right. Then pause and take a deep breath. Look at the customer and say this exactly...

> **Mr Customer, I know this is a lot of information about your vehicle,**
> **DO YOU HAVE ANY QUESTIONS FOR ME?!?**

Now you are done with the MPI Presentation. The customer will now answer your question. In almost every case the customer will say one of two statements.

> **_Customer #1:_** Yes. How much are those _____ items that failed.

Notice what just happened. The multi-point inspection item that failed is now important to the customer and it is now a primary concern. The customer is a buyer. The service advisor remains a loyal advocate and is simply taking an order from the customer who is directing them to make a purchase.

Reviewing the results is the key. We advised the customer at writeup that they would know everything about their car when they leave today. Now it's important to tell them the results.

> **_Customer #2:_** WOW, that was the best report anyone has ever given me. Thank you.
> **_Service Advisor:_** Would you like a quote to have those failed items taken care of today?

That happens to be the next step in the MPI Process.

> Ask the customer, "Would you like a quote to have these failed items taken care of today?"

Naturally the customer is going to approve your request. Asking permission keeps the customer in control of the process. So far the service advisor has done everything that they have promised, so a quote would simply be the next step.

The final step to the MPI process is to ask the customer...

> How would you like your quote? Would you prefer it to be a grand total or itemized in order of importance?

The customer is now going to tell you exactly how to present the items. Remember the ways discussed earlier.

Grand Total • *RIM* • *Line-By-Line*

BAM! The customer will tell you how to sell them!

Now there are a couple of advanced next steps if the service advisor is ready for them. Once the customer informs the service advisor of the way to present the items, the service advisor can say this...

> Great! Let me leave the MPI Report with you. I will go to my desk and prepare a customized estimate for you. Give me about five minutes and I'll show you the numbers and review them as you requested so you can feel comfortable.

The reason for this is simple. Most of the time, the service advisor is going at a fast pace. The customer is typically much slower. Give the customer a few minutes of private time and they will close themselves on the important items. Often this time is just what the customer needs to make a decision. Naturally, the service advisor has the quote prepared at the desk. Walk back to the service desk and grab a sip of water, smoke a cigarette or get prepared for the presentation. Then head back to the customer and make the sales presentation.

Reality sets in, and the service advisor may not have an extra five minutes. So be prepared with a complete quote itemized and categorized to present to the customer.

> Great! I have taken the liberty to prepare a customized quote for you. Let me show you the numbers and review them as you requested so you can feel comfortable.

The MPI Process in Review

1. Ask For Permission to Perform the Multi-Point Inspection

2. Complete the Primary Concern - Sold

3. Ask For Permission to Review the Results of the MPI

4. Review the Results of the MPI

   - ✓ Name - Year/Make/Model/ Specific Mileage 123456

   - ✓ Use Pass/Fail

5. Ask "Do you have any Questions"

6. Ask "Would you like a Quote"

7. Ask "How would you like your Quote"

   - ✓ Grand Total

   - ✓ Prioritize in Order of Importance

   - ✓ Line By Line

Master Tip!

As a service advisor there are many tricks to the trade. There are many ways to plant the seed for the customer. One example of this is to describe items to a customer in the waiting room who does not require a specific service. For instance...

Customer #1 has 30,000 miles on their vehicle. Customer #2 has 80,000 miles on the vehicle and is going to need coolant services such as hoses and belts. Customer #1 does not need these items. A service advisor may educate customer #1 about the importance of coolant work at higher mileage.

> Mr. Customer, your coolant system passes our vehicle inspection today. In the future, say around 60-80,000 miles, your coolant system will require attention. We inspect the hoses for pliability. It is important for your hoses to be soft and pliable, not too soft to cause a leak and not brittle enough to crack. No need to worry now; we will be monitoring this for you as a part of our commitment to protecting your investment.

Customer #2 is listening attentively and begins to think about the hoses on that vehicle with 80,000 miles. This approach is *mastering the waiting room.*

Power Words

The words used in sales presentations can have a dramatic affect on the presentation. Some words can influence the sale positively and other words can diminish the presentation. It is important to choose the words carefully. Using the right word will set the service sales person up for a successful transaction. Using the wrong word or the right word incorrectly can have a devastating effect on the sale. Often the sales person is unaware of the psychology of the words utilized in their pitch. Even the most seasoned professional often confuses the language. As the professional service advisor studies the words, make mental notes of the best words that will positively affect the sale.

Review each of these words below, listen and hear how they sound in a sentence.

Power Words to Use

- ✓ **Required** - An oil change is required every 5000 Miles - "Required" states that it is a must to do.

- ✓ **Now** - An oil change is required NOW. "Now" implies a sense of urgency.

- ✓ **Important** - It is important to replace your brakes. "Important" tells the severity of the job.

- ✓ **Encourage** - I encourage you to do this now. "Encourage" supports the decision.

- ✓ **Vital** - It is vital to change your oil every 5000 miles. Vital ups the severity of the job.

- ✓ **Necessary** - It is necessary to replace your transmission fluid every 30,000 miles. "Necessary" indicates the importance of the repair.

- ✓ **Expert** - My expert technician will be working on your car. Everyone wants an expert to fix the problem.

- ✓ **Keep** - Keep your vehicle maintained. - Most people hate change; keep your vehicle the same as it is now... in great shape.

- ✓ **Just out of curiosity** - I am just curious, what is keeping you from having this service done today. This phrase softens the statement. It keeps the service advisor in rapport with the customer.

Power words to avoid

- ✓ **Maybe** - Maybe you should change your oil.

- ✓ **Kind Of** - It's kind of important.

- ✓ **Might** - we might get this done today.

- ✓ **Estimate** - we will get close to a price.

- ✓ **OEM** - This is an acronym, and most customers do not know what OEM stands for.

- ✓ **RO** - Another acronym. Most customers believe this is dealer talk.

- ✓ **Should** - You should change your oil every 5000 miles. Stop telling people what to do. Most people do not like to be told what to do: especially by technicians. When we tell people what to do, they often do the opposite. Some people say, do not "should" all over your customers. Do not tell them what to do. A wall goes up between the customer and the service advisor.

- ✓ **Recommend** - I recommend that you get your brakes replaced. Recommending items make a service advisor a sales person. The customer is looking for an advocate.

A better way...

There are items that require attention on your vehicle today. Some require attention immediately, and other items will require attention in the near future. It is important to replace your brakes today.

Should = Important
Recommend = Requires Attention

Compare these statements.

❌ I recommend brakes
VS
✔️ **Your brakes require attention**

❌ My technician recommends an alignment
VS
✔️ **Your tires require attention. An alignment is important, because….**

❌ I recommend a 30k service
VS
✔️ **Your vehicle requires its scheduled maintenance now**

❌ You should replace your brakes today
VS
✔️ **It is important to replace your brakes today**

❌ You should do an alignment today
VS
✔️ **An alignment is important to protect your investment**

❌ I recommend a 30k Service
VS
✔️ **A major service is required today**

Choosing the words for presentations is vital to ensure the walls between the service advisor and the customer remain broken down. Often service advisors will either tell a customer what to do or try to sell them something. Both of these approaches damage the relationship and subliminally make the customer say no. Educate the customer on the importance of the item, and they will buy from the service advisor.

3 Creating Amazing Presentations

It is time to start making real professional sales presentations to the customer. The presentations made to the customer must be enthusiastic in nature to draw the customer to want to make a purchase. The customer must see value in the work the technician is selling. The customer must also feel as if they cannot go anywhere else to receive this type of work. It all starts with an amazing presentation.

Selling in the service department is an educational process. Most service advisors want the customer to feel like they are in control and educated about the vehicle system, service or part that requires attention. As well, most advisors prefer to be considered a consultant or advocate for the customer. This comes by making a presentation or educating the customer about the repair or service. If the customer receives enough information in the right way, they are most likely to make a purchase.

It is time to talk about the ABC's of educating the customer.

Educate

Educate the customer on the item that requires attention. Advise the customer why this needs to be replaced or serviced. Then provide the customer benefits for making a purchase. The service advisor should also provide a brief description of the repair or service to build enough value so that the only answer can be a yes.

The ABCs of Educating

A = The Item that requires **ATTENTION**

B = The reason it is **BEING** replaced

C = The **CUSTOMER** Benefits

D = **DESCRIPTION** of the Service or Repair

In any service and repair transaction, it is important to identify the items that need to be replaced or serviced. This is the item that requires attention.

It is also important to educate the customer on the reasons 'why' the item is being serviced or replaced. The service advisor must create a **need** for the customer to make a purchase. Remember the objection, where the customer has "no need", this is how the service advisor creates the need.

In the movie "The Wolf of Wall Street", Jordan Belford showed the group of sales people how to sell a pen. He took the pen away from the rookies, and then he created a need to sign an important document. What choice did the team have but to buy a pen from him at a greatly inflated price?

Once the item is described in enough detail so the customer knows the real reason (need) for the service or repair, the service advisor can then educate the customer on the benefits of having this repair completed. Remember the benefits to the customer are...

✓ *Safety*   ✓ *Reliability - Dependability*

✓ *Performance*   ✓ *Protecting the Investment*

The service advisor can provide a brief description of the repair or service to build enough value so that the only answer can be a yes. It is vital to educate the customer on the high points of the job to ensure the customer has all the information about the repair. In many cases it's comparable to a warranty repair for the manufacturer. The service advisor must tell the auto manufacturer the steps necessary to complete the warranty job in order to be paid the full amount. Consider doing this for the customer. Provide the important details to allow the customer to understand the amount of complexity and detail involved in every repair. Yes, even including oil changes. This allows the customer to understand the VALUE of the service.

In the following examples, read to understand the differences in the sales approach.

> *As a 21-year veteran service advisor, it is great to go back to the basics for success. Creating a need for the customer is vital to the sale. The ABCs are the foundation to make more money. I always pick up new information in every class. Steve Shaw Training always gets our team focused on selling.* **Brooks Falzone –** Honda Service Advisor

Typical Sales Pitch

Service Advisor: Your alternator is bad and needs to be replaced. It's $695. I can have this done today.

Customer: Can I get a discount?

ABC Amazing Presentation

The item that requires ATTENTION today is the Alternator

The reason it is **BEING** replaced is that your alternator failed the performance test and is only charging to 9 Volts vs. 14.6

The **(CUSTOMER)** benefits to you are that your car will be reliable and dependable. This repair will save you money in the future. - _Safety, Proper starting every day in all weather, long life of the battery, preventing costly repairs in the future. Peace of mind._

The **DESCRIPTION** of the repair is: To replace this alternator we will need to remove the upper engine cover, remove the belts and power steering pump to access the alternator. This is a complex repair that requires a special tool for re-alignment of the components. A (insert make) technician is the most qualified to install this important part.

ABC Amazing Presentation Example in practice...

The Item that requires attention today is your alternator. The reason that it needs to be replaced is that your alternator failed the performance test. Your alternator is charging to 9 volts, whereas a properly-working alternator charges to 14.6 volts. By having this replaced today, you can be sure the car will be reliable and dependable for your family. In fact, this will prevent costly repairs in the future, which will save you lots of money. The way we do this repair here at Hometown Motors is like this: my expert technician will remove the upper engine cover, remove the belts and brackets to access the hidden components. He will then remove and reinstall the Toyota (Specific Manufacturer) part. This is a complex repair that requires the use of Toyota special tools and reprogramming. It is important that only a Toyota Technician installs this vital part on your vehicle, because....

As you can read, the ABC example is a much more professional approach to the sales presentation. The customer understands why the alternator is needed. The customer understands what is in it for them (Safety, Reliability, Saving Money). Finally, the customer understands the complexity of the repair and why a Toyota Technician is the best suited to install this part.

In this ABC example, the price is not discussed, nor is it important.

Price is not the issue here. The customer is highly unlikely to ask for a discount due to the nature of the work.

The customer will see and hear the VALUE of what is being sold

Typical Brake Job Sales Pitch

<u>**Service Advisor:**</u> My technician noticed that your brakes are down metal to metal. We recommend brakes today. Your cost - parts and labor is $229 plus tax.

<u>**Customer:**</u> I can have my mechanic fix those brakes; just take care of the oil change. Thanks.

ABC Amazing Presentation Scenario in practice...

What Item Requires ATTENTION? Front Brake Pads

WHY is this item BEING replaced? Front Pads worn below specifications; your pads are at 3mm. Manufacturer suggests replacement at 4mm. New Pads start at 8mm.

What are the CUSTOMER BENEFITS for the Action? Safety, shortened stopping distance, extending the life of the rotors, preventing costly repairs of new rotors, peace of mind.

Provide a DESCRIPTION of the service or repair. - Remove the wheels calipers and connecting hardware to access the rotors, remove the brake rotors, measure them with a micrometer. Once it is established that the rotors are above the manufacturer's specification, we can resurface the rotors and remove the warped and discoloration of the rotors. Make an accurate cut our (insert make) brake lathe. Once this is completed we will reinstall the components, adjust to proper (insert make) specification. Provide the correct finish to the rotors, road test 5 miles to ensure the vehicle concern is corrected.

ABC Amazing Presentation

The Item that requires attention is your front brake pads. The reason they need to be replaced is that your brakes measure 3mm. The auto manufacturer requires brakes to be replaced at 4mm, and new brakes start at 8mm. The benefits to you are that your vehicle will stop as designed, keeping your car reliable. This will save you money on additional brake rotors, and you can have peace of mind that your family will be safe on the road. The way we do this at Hometown Motors is, my technician will remove the calipers and hardware to access the brakes. He will measure and resurface the rotors. This will give you the hard brake pedal you are accustomed to. He will then install new factory pads. Finally my expert technician will road test the vehicle and ensure the best braking performance.

This presentation provides the customer exactly what is already being done in a complete brake service at the dealership. The point of utilizing our ABCs is to educate the customer on the higher quality of work at the dealership. The need to discuss cost is not a factor (yet) in this brake service. In this presentation the service advisor builds value and professionalism.

Oil Change

Now, imagine an oil change scenario. Imagine how much money the dealership spends annually to attract customers in for a basic oil service. The spend is dramatic, most likely in the tens of thousands of dollars. Now for a minute visualize the typical oil change presentation.

Typical Oil Change Sales Pitch

Customer: I am here for my oil change.

Service Advisor: Its $39.99.

Customer: Do you have a coupon; that sounds expensive.

An ABC scenario is much different.

What is the item that requires **ATTENTION**? The scheduled maintenance service - oil change and tire rotation - most likely.

Why is this **BEING** replaced or serviced? The manufacturer requires the scheduled maintenance.

What are the **CUSTOMER** Benefits for this service? Protect Investment, Maintain Warranty Compliance, Keep Vehicle Reliable and Dependable. Keep family safe on the road.

Provide a **DESCRIPTION** of the Service. Expert technician will drain and replace engine oil with factory-approved oil. Replace with factory filter with check valve to ensure proper oil circulation. Rotate Tires and Perform MPI. Car wash.

ABC Amazing Presentation Example in practice...

The Item that requires attention today is your 5000 Mile Service. The reason it needs to be completed is that the manufacturer requires this service based on your time and mileage. The benefits to you are that our service will ensure the safety and reliability of your vehicle. My expert technician will drain the engine oil and replace it with factory-approved oil. This allows maximum protection during the intervals between oil changes. He will replace the oil filter with a factory filter, and ours actually has a check valve to ensure that on start up you have oil circulating immediately throughout your engine. He will then rotate your tires to help them last a long time. We provide all of our customers a complimentary Multi-Point Inspection (or health check). This will ensure your peace of mind for the lifetime of your vehicle. By the way, we will have this done in 45 minutes or less. I can even get your car washed in that same time.

Diagnostic Charge

The diagnostic charge is one of the most difficult items to sell to the customer. Make no mistake about this, the service advisor must SELL the diagnosis. Many service advisors will say how easy this is to GET from the customer. A better way is to educate the customer on the benefits of a diagnostic charge.

The diagnostic charge is slightly different from the other scenarios, as the customer only wants one thing from this inspection. The customer wants an accurate quote to have the vehicle repaired. One can make the argument that they want the accurate quote to keep their vehicle safe on the road, reliable and dependable, achieve better performance, or to protect their investment. This is arguably true. However, it is best to present the accurate quote as the benefit.

Typical Diagnostic Sales Pitch

Customer: My check engine light is on.

Service Advisor: The diagnostic charge is $99.99. If you have the work done, we will roll the cost into the repair. If you choose not to have it done then we charge you $99.99 to pay our technician.

Customer: WOW! That's expensive, but I guess go ahead.

An ABC scenario is much different.

What is the item that requires ATTENTION? The Diagnostic Inspection

Why is this BEING replaced or serviced? The Check Engine Light is flashing on the dash

What are the CUSTOMER Benefits for this service? Accurate Quote

Provide a DESCRIPTION of the Service. Verify the concern, test drive, check for TSB and recalls through the VIN System, Scan System for DTC, Pinpoint test, Follow manufacturer trouble tree, create quote

---

ABC Amazing Presentation Example in practice...

In order to provide you an accurate quote to address the check engine light, my technician will complete the following steps:

- ✓ Inspect and Verify the Concern

- ✓ Test Drive

- ✓ Run the vehicle through our VIN System and evaluate any Technical Service Bulletins (TSB) that apply to your car.

- ✓ Perform a Diagnostic Scan of the complex computer system and look for trouble codes (DTCs)

- ✓ Perform Pinpoint Tests

- ✓ Contact the technician assistance center if necessary

- ✓ Perform any additional tests as required by the manufacturer

- ✓ Develop an accurate quote for the repair.

We can have this done by 12:00 today. The total cost is $99.99. May I have your permission to perform this important service now?

The focus of the presentation is about the complex work the technician is performing. The main point is not whether the customer will get their money back. The benefit of the service is the accurate quote, not rolling it into the repair (which in many cases is a lie.)

The purpose of each one of these examples is to point out how a presentation can sound to the customer. Value overcomes cost in this type of presentation. Customers focus less on the price and more on the value of the serivce. Often customers approve the sale without knowing the price.

Adding the Cost

In every sales presentation the last item to discuss before the close is the price. For instance, the ABCs with the price added will look like this...

A = Item that requires **ATTENTION**

B = Why is this **BEING** replaced

C = What are the **CUSTOMER** Benefits

D = Provide a **DESCRIPTION** of the sale

$ = Add the Cost of the Service

The cost of the item is added in near the end of the sales presentation. Anything the service advisor wants to discuss with the customer must be said prior to the cost being discussed. The moment price is brought up by the service advisor, price becomes the issue. The customer stops listening to the presentation and begins to decide financially if they want the service.

Imagine when a customer calls the dealership on the telephone and asks, "How much is an oil change"? The service advisor almost instinctively says the price is $29.99. The customer's next thought is, " WOW, that's expensive". The service advisor then proceeds to describe all the features and benefits of the serivce. This is to no avail. The customer is focused on the price.

Remember to advise the customer of all important components of the sale. This includes, Rental Cars, Completion Time, Parts Availablity, etc...

A = Item that requires **ATTENTION**
B = Why is this **BEING** replaced
C = What are the **CUSTOMER** Benefits
D = Provide a **DESCRIPTION** of the sale
$ = Add the Cost of the Service

Closing the Sale

Many service advisors like to point out their sales prowees by saying they always assume the sale. Assume, Assume, Assume is what some sales trainers teach. There are many instances where an argument for assuming the sale is a good technique. In the serivce department this is not one of them.

Here is why... would you like someone to do this to you?

Most times when service advisors assume the sale, they are doing this because they are not sure if there is enough value presented to the customer. They assume the sale and try a hard close to get the customer in agreement.

Have you ever had a customer come to pick up their vehicle and say to the cashier, "I did not authorize this"? This typically happens because the customer did not agree to the sale. Or they certainly did not understand what they were pressured into purchasing. Assuming the sale is a pressure tactic.

Customer Retention is defined in many ways. The easiest way to define retention is to evaluate how often the customer returns to the serivce department for customer pay items. Some manufacturers measure retention based on one or two visits per year to the serivce departments. This is an indicator of the ability to sell a new vehicle to the customer. Most dealers place a higher value on selling the next car than hard selling a customer in the drive.

The service advisor in fact is a sales person. This sales person is tasked with many responsiblities, and the most important job criteria for a service adivsor is customer retention. Car dealers want to the opportunity to sell more cars. Car dealers sell more service by having customers return.

The most effective and customer-driven approach is to simply ask for the sale. Here is a typical example.

May I have your permission to take care of this service today?

Often service advisors will want a stronger closing statement or question to increase the importance of the repair. Here are a few examples to ask for the sale and make it powerful.

Remember The Power Words:

IMPORTANT, VITAL, NECESSARY, NOW, EXPERT

May I have your permission to take care of this **IMPORTANT** *service today?*

May I have your permission to take care of this **IMPORTANT** *service* **NOW**?

Would you like my **EXPERT** *technician to take care of this service today?*

Would you like my **EXPERT** *technician to take care of this* **IMPORTANT** *service* **NOW**?

Adding a power word or two to the closing can increase the urgency and importance of the repair. This will ensure that the service advisor maintains the rapport with the customer and shows the need.

The service advisor politely asks permission to do the work. Utilizing the ABC Value Selling Approach, it is easy to know how and when to ask for the sale.

A = Item that requires **ATTENTION**

B = Why is this **BEING** replaced

C = What are the **CUSTOMER** Benefits

D = Provide a **DESCRIPTION** of the sale

$ = Add the Cost of the Service

Close = Ask Permission for the Work

Asking permission is customer friendly. The ABC approach, in fact, keeps the service advisor on track for the sales as well.

Over the years, many a service advisor has talked themselves right out of the repvair sale. This happens because the advisor is unsure of the order, the steps and the way to present a sale to the customer. Many times the advisor is all over the map. Presentations look like A, $, B, Close, C.

The best approach to every sales is to be consistent and present every sale the same way. It has been said that every sale in the service department is the same. This is the most truthful statement in the book. Every sale is the same. The sale starts at A and ends at Close.

Each item or sale may require different verbiage and skill and priorities for the customer, but remember: every sale is the same.

A = Item that requires **ATTENTION**

B = Why is this **BEING** replaced

C = What are the CUSTOMER Benefits

D = Provide a **DESCRIPTION** of the sale

$ = Add the Cost of the Service

Close = Ask Permission for the Work

Here is a sample word track document that can be used on ANY item for sale in the dealership. This word track outline allows the service advisor to consistently make an amazing presentation.

The item that requires attention today is
_____.

The reason this needs to be serviced is
_____.

The benefits to you are

1) _____

2) _____

3) _____

Safety
Reliable / Dependable
Performance
Protect Investment

The way we do this at our dealership is
_____

The total cost is _____

May I have your permission to take care of this important service now?

An Amazing Presentation

The item that requires attention today is your front brake pads.

The reason they need to be replaced is that your brake pads are worn below 3mm. The manufacturer requires replacement at 4mm and new brake pads start at 8mm.

The benefits of new brakes today are 1) your family will be safe on the road again 2) you will save money on future repairs of costly rotors, this will help protect your investment and finally, 3) you will have that braking performance that you have always relied on since new.

The way we perform this service here at Hometown Motors is like this.. My expert technician is going to disassemble your brake calipers and replace the old pads with high quality factory value line pads; he will then clean and lubricate all the connecting hardware. He will top off the brake fluid, bleed any air in the system as necessary. Once this is complete he will road test your vehicle 5 miles to ensure the brakes are seated properly and you have a like new pedal and the system is quality checked.

The total cost for this important repair is $229.99.

May I have your permission to perform this vital service now?

Creating Amazing Presentations - Conclusion

Selling is simply an educational process from the service advisor to the customer. The professional service advisor will make an attempt to educate the customer on all service sales. It is vital for the service advisor to utilize the same process for each and every sales attempt with the customer. This will provide the customer a clear understanding of the items that require attention. This will remove any obstacles towards the sale beginning with the NEED.

Once the need is established, the service advisor can present the customer benefits and then describe the actual process being completed on the customer's vehicle.

This is the value for the customer. The customer will understand the benefits to them. They will also have a true picture of the service being performed. Once this is fully spelled out to the customer, then and only then can the service advisor present the cost or the customer investment. Finally, the service advisor can close the sale. In the process described in Master of the Waiting Room, the service advisor can simply ask the customer's permission for this important service. When the service advisor uses the power words, it drives the sense of urgency. Customers logically say "YES" to the sale.

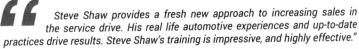

Steve Shaw provides a fresh new approach to increasing sales in the service drive. His real life automotive experiences and up-to-date practices drive results. Steve Shaw's training is impressive, and highly effective."

Stephanie Wilson – Corporate Service Drive Trainer

4. Overcoming Objections

In most training classes, service advisors become excited to talk about overcoming objections. Service advisors are looking for the magic bullet to get a customer to switch from NO to YES. There is NO magic word to make this happen. Service Advisors CAN, however, through smart work and some persuasion turn a "No" into a purchase. Remember, in all cases the most important item to understand is that the service advisor has a current relationship with the customer. This relationship can be 5 minutes, or 25 years. One sale is not worth damaging this relationship. The relationship is maintained by using the correct approach to the customer. Maintaining the relationship is the right thing to become excited about.

The right approach to any sale can prevent objections from ever surfacing. The reason the author has spent so much time discussing value is due to the always-present VALUE PROPOSITION. Value must overcome cost for any transaction to be successful. Value is the key in service for the customer to make a purchase.

- ✓ Typical objections heard in the service department.
- ✓ I do not have enough money.
- ✓ I do not have enough time today.
- ✓ I am selling the car.
- ✓ I am leasing the vehicle.
- ✓ I do not need it.
- ✓ I do not want it.
- ✓ I can get it cheaper elsewhere.
- ✓ I have a coupon for Jiffy Lube.
- ✓ My brother is a mechanic.
- ✓ It costs too much.
- ✓ I do not like you.
- ✓ I do not trust you.
- ✓ I only deal with men.
- ✓ I only deal with women.
- ✓ Car dealerships rip me off.
- ✓ I live too far from here.
- ✓ You never call me back.
- ✓ I have to call my spouse.
- ✓ I only use you for warranty repairs.
- ✓ I have my own mechanic.
- ✓ I want a discount.
- ✓ Many, Many More.

In the service department there are usually only two primary objections for the customer, time and money. The most popular objection that the service advisor focuses on is MONEY. This is the objection that service advisors hear in their minds the most. This is the objection that nearly every customer has for not purchasing today at the dealership.

With enough practice a service advisor can overcome this objection. However, to become an expert with MONEY it's important to understand the process for lowering the walls and becoming one with the customer. It is easy to push a customer into a sale. It is even easier to give a customer "buyer's remorse". The right approach to objections will allow the service advisor to maintain the desired relationship.

Research shows the #1 reason a customer defects from the dealership is TRUST. The most common real reasons that a customer does not purchase from a dealership is...

1. Trust	6.
2. Convenience	97.
3. Value	98.
4.	99.
5.	100. Money

Trust is the number one reason. The customer does not trust the dealership. Often this trust comes in the perception of overcharging. The customer does not understand the repair or feels like the dealership is ripping them off for service, just because they can. This is why creating a trusting relationship is the most important thread in the dealership customer experience. The service advisor must follow through on call back times, cost structure, promise and completion times. When the service advisor creates a trusting relationship, the customer will lower their defenses and be more willing to make a purchase. When the customer has trust in the service advisor, this is certainly value as well. Create trust and sell more.

Convenience is a close second reason for not purchasing service at the dealership. Take a moment and recall all the customers who come in for an oil change and wait for hours on end to have a simple service completed. What customer wants to wait to have service on the dealership time and then have additional work done on their day off?

Most customers want to have service now. Most are willing to spend money if the dealership makes it convenient for them. If the dealership makes a customer wait more than 15 minutes for an MPI, the chances of a sale diminish greatly. The longer the wait time for an answer on the repair and items that require attention, the less likely a customer will make a purchase.

Consider the wait time for an appointment. Any customer that waits for more than 24 hours for an appointment is also inconvenienced. This too lowers the customer's willingness to make a purchase. At all times, making it convenient is important in the sales process. The more convenient, the easier the sale becomes. Imagine if the dealership could service vehicles in a right-now situation. The customer would be willing to wait while the repairs or service are being handled. Sales go up. Declines go down as well, along with rental car expense. Making it convenient is certainly value for the customer. Value goes up, sales go up.

Value is the third reason. Seventy percent of people buy value vs. cost. The argument can be made that trust and convenience are components of Value. When a service advisor attempts to build trust, this provides value to the customer. The same can be said for convenience - the more convenient the more value. Hence, value is the only reason a customer does not purchase from the dealership. Building value in the products and services that the dealership provides is of the highest importance for the dealership service advisor. Using the ABCs to create value is the best approach. This too removes many of the objections. The customer becomes more willing to make a purchase. The entire point of this book so far is to demonstrate to the service advisor how to build value. The LEAD approach to overcoming objections is merely another tool, although advanced, on how to build value.

Steve Shaw Training shows you how to accept customers properly, listen to them, and helps you understand their needs so that they feel comfortable when coming into your dealership! The approach helps customers buy more service."

Richard Anderson – Jaguar Service Advisor

LEAD - Overcoming Objections Approach

The LEAD approach to objection handling is a proven and effective way to build value and maintain the relationship the service advisor has built with the customer. This relationship may be over the course of years or simply a few minutes. Keeping the relationship is the key to retention. The service advisor can sell service for high dollar and retain customers.

LEAD is an acronym to help the service advisor remember the steps.

L = **Listen** (And Restate the Objection)

E = Show **Empathy** to the customer

A = **Ask** Clarifying Questions

D = **Determine** a Solution to the objection

For Example

Objection = Not enough time

L = I understand you feel you do not have enough time today to complete the brake repair...

E = I can appreciate that, your time is extremely valuable; it seems there is never enough time in the day to get everything done...

A = May I ask you a question - If I could get you alternative transportation, would that work for you?

D = Great! let's go back to my desk, and I'll get you a car to drive.

It appears simple on the surface. The point of this process is to provide the service advisor a complete step-by-step solution to overcoming objections.

Listen

In the first step L is to listen clearly to the objection given by the customer. Whatever the objection presented, the service advisor must restate it back to the customer. In fact the service advisor can "parrot" or repeat the exact objection. It is vital for the service advisor to **ACKNOWLEDGE** the customer's objection. Once the customer agrees to this acknowledgement with a "Yes", then and only then can the service advisor move forward and show empathy for the customer's concern.

Here are some responses to the objections below...

- ✓ **I do not have enough money** - I understand you feel you do not have the money today
- ✓ **I do not have enough time today** - I understand you feel you do not have enough time today
- ✓ **I am selling the car** - I hear you: you are selling your car
- ✓ **I am leasing vehicle** - great; you are leasing your car
- ✓ **I can get it cheaper elsewhere** - sure; I understand you feel you can get it cheaper somewhere else
- ✓ **I have a coupon for Jiffy Lube** - I hear you, you have a coupon for Jiffy Lube
- ✓ **My brother is a mechanic** - that's handy; your brother is a mechanic
- ✓ **It cost too much** - I hear you: you feel it costs too much
- ✓ **I do not like you** - I understand you do not like me
- ✓ **I do not trust you** - I understand you do not trust me
- ✓ **I only deal with men** - I understand you only deal with men
- ✓ **I only deal with women** - I understand you only deal with women
- ✓ **Car dealerships rip me off** - I understand you feel car dealerships rip you off
- ✓ **I live too far from here** - I hear that you feel you live to far from here
- ✓ **You never call me back** - I understand you feel I never call you back
- ✓ **I have to call my spouse** - I hear you: you need to call your spouse
- ✓ **I only use you for warranty repairs** - ok:you only use us for warranty repairs
- ✓ **I have my own mechanic** - that's great: you have your own mechanic
- ✓ **I want a discount** - I understand; you want a discount

The service advisor must restate the objection to acknowledge the correct objection. This allows the service advisor and the customer to be on the same page. Listening and acknowledging begins to put the customer at ease. This too allows the service advisor to move forward with the next step.

Empathy

This is where the service advisor must align themselves with the customers. The service advisor must demonstrate to the customer that they are on the same page or that they are just like the customer. The service advisor must ALIGN themself with the customer in this step. This is like the service advisor saying, "I am just like you". Demonstrating empathy can be more difficult than it seems sometimes. In many cases of objections a "wall" goes up between the service advisor and the customer. The customer says NO!

BAM!

A wall goes up!

The easy way out is to say OK. I'll get your car ready for you. The right way is to put yourself in the customer's shoes and attempt to overcome the objection. By showing empathy, what is happening is the service advisor is pushing the wall down and sitting side-by-side with the customer.

Books have been written on empathy. The point of empathy here in Master of the Waiting Room is to give you deliberate steps to selling service to increase CSI, Retention, and of course, Repair Order Performance. Performing at a higher level starts with the ability to overcome objections. As a result, the service advisor's paycheck will improve dramatically. Empathy is simply the ability for one person to relate to another. Demonstrating empathy shows one person that the other is just like them. Empathy shows an understanding and even a caring for another's plight.

The point of demonstrating empathy is for the service advisor to push down that wall and be on the same side as the customer. Demonstrating empathy allows the service advisor to show the customer that they are willing to work together to find the best solution for the customer. Creating an empathetic situation allows the customer to see how the service advisor is an advocate for them. The service advisor is not just a pushy sales person. The service advisor can demonstrate empathy in many ways.

Obviously body language and tone of voice apply in every situation. By using the correct posture and tone, a service advisor can turn any situation into a positive and save the customer and often the sale. Some service advisors will get down on the same level and look eye-to-eye with the customer. The best approach with a female is to be face-to-face. The best approach with a male is to be side to side. Using body language to create empathy is a powerful tool the service advisor toolbox.

Below are some objections and some empathetic responses.

- ✓ **I do not have enough money** - it is important to get the best value for your dollar

---

Any time a customer speaks about money, the professional service advisor changes the conversation to value for $

- ✓ **I do not have enough time today** - I too never seem to have enough time to get everything done
- ✓ **I am selling the car** - I just sold my car; sometimes this can be a trying task
- ✓ **I am leasing the vehicle** - leasing is a great way to get a new car every few years. It also has great business tax advantages
- ✓ **I can get it cheaper elsewhere** - I too like to get the best value for my dollar
- ✓ **I have a coupon for Jiffy Lube** - I am a coupon clipper too
- ✓ **My brother is a mechanic** - it sure is great to have someone in the business you can trust
- ✓ **It costs too much** - I am always looking to get the best value for my dollar
- ✓ **I do not like you** - it is important to do business with people you like and trust
- ✓ **I do not trust you** - it is important to do business with people you like and trust
- ✓ **I only deal with men** - it is important to do business with people you like and trust
- ✓ **I only deal with women** - it is important to do business with people you like and trust
- ✓ **Car dealerships rip me off** - many of my best customers used to feel the same way
- ✓ **I live too far from here** - your time is very valuable
- ✓ **You never call me back** - I know how important your schedule is
- ✓ **I have to call my spouse** - I call my spouse on important items as well
- ✓ **I only use you for warranty repairs** - I too like to get the best value for my dollar
- ✓ **I have my own mechanic** - it's great to have someone in the business you can trust
- ✓ **I want a discount** - I too like to get the best value for my dollar

Empathy comes in many forms. Often the same statement works for many different objections. The point is for the customer to feel that you are on their side. Often it's not always about the service advisor. It can be about other people who are just like the customer as well. Demonstrate empathy to align with the customer. This will put the service advisor and the customer side-by-side in the sales process. The concern will be there for both to resolve together. The service advisor and the customer will attempt to solve the problem together. The customer will feel like they have an advocate in the sales process, not a pushy sales person. Often the customer will open up about their real situation and solutions can be found.

ASK Clarifying Questions

Asking questions leads to answers. The next chapter begins a discussion on how to question the customer. It is important to remember that the service advisor has shown the ability to acknowledge and align themselves with the customer. The questions that develop become a conversation with the customer. When learning about how to question a customer, it may appear to be robotic. The seasoned professional makes it seem natural. The conversation opens up about the true desires of the customer and how to make the repair a fit for the customer. The service advisor is seeking clarification about the objection. What is it going to take to resolve the objection? In most cases the service advisor has made an amazing presentation. The customer has said, "NO THANKS". Now is the time to ask questions to probe and clarify the objection. If the service advisor asks the right question, the customer will either tell them the way to sell them or the service advisor will get the customer to realize the importance of the repair.

Here are some sample questions to ASK when confronted with the objection...

```
━━━━━━━━━━━ No Time ━━━━━━━━━━━
  ✔  How much time do you have?

  ✔  Would you be interested in a loaner vehicle?

  ✔  Would you be interested in a rental vehicle?

  ✔  If I could get you a ride home, would that work?
```

This one is fairly simple to overcome if the service advisor follows the process. Find out how much time the customer actually has today. Ask the customer if they are interested in alternative transportation.

No Money

- ✓ Did you have a budget in mind for your repairs today (How much money do you have?)?
- ✓ Would you be interested in our "90 day same as cash" program?
- ✓ Are you interested in an aftermarket alternative part?
- ✓ Is there anyone who can help you with the repair cost?
- ✓ What is important to you in your auto repair today?

Remember in the LEAD process, the service advisor has demonstrated empathy. The caring service advisor can ask a customer any question if it helps solve the problem.

"Your safety is important to me, and as I explained, your brakes are down to the rivets (1mm). This can cause a small maintenance to turn into a major repair in a few miles. Is there someone who can help you with this today?

Costs Too Much

- ✓ Did you have a budget in mind for your auto repair?
- ✓ Are you aware of the benefits of our service?
- ✓ How much were you looking to invest in your repairs today?
- ✓ What makes you feel like this costs too much?
- ✓ What brings you to the dealership?
- ✓ Has anyone ever told you how we price our service?

Cheaper Elsewhere

- ✓ Where can you get it cheaper?
- ✓ Do you have a written quote?
- ✓ Are you aware of the differences between the dealer service and the other guys?
- ✓ Are you interested in an aftermarket alternative part?
- ✓ What brings you to us for inspection?

- ✓ How long has he been your mechanic?
- ✓ Who is your mechanic?
- ✓ What brought you to us?
- ✓ What do you like about your mechanic?

Most people are expecting the service advisor to talk negatively about their mechanic. The better way is to ask questions about their mechanic. Take an interest in the customer. Actually praise them and ask why they came to the dealership for inspection.

How to soften your questions

In order not to pressure a customer, it is best to soften the approach. This is done by saying...

- ✓ May I ask you a question?
- ✓ Just out of curiosity, what, why, how....?

Asking questions will help the professional service advisor find the clarification they need to overcome the specific objection. Asking questions is a polite way to find out the necessary information. Apply the body language techniques from above as well. The customer will appreciate how the service advisor took an interest in the solution, not just the sale. Probing questions show sincerity and move the conversation forward to a desired outcome.

Determine a Solution

Service Advisors are natural problem solvers. That is what service advisors do best. The problem is often that service advisors rush to solve the problem, and that can turn off a customer. Determining a solution is the easy part of handling the objection. When a service advisor jumps to a solution after being told "NO", the customer can get offended or worse feel like the service advisor is just a sales person. The customer feels like the service advisor just wants to make a sale, not having the customer's interest at heart. The LEAD approach puts determining a solution as the last step. This is frustrating to the service advisor, because "hurry up and sell" is the way of life on the drive. The better way is to actually LEAD a customer to solving their own concern by asking questions and setting the stage for a solution.

Real World Example - Costs too much!

Service Advisor - **(L)** I understand you feel the dealership just costs too much.

(E) I can appreciate that; I am always trying to get the best value for my money as well.

(A) May I ask you a question? Has anyone ever told you how we price our work?

Well, here at Hometown Motors, we believe in being competitive in the marketplace. We know that we are not the cheapest place for repairs, but we also know based on our research that we are not the most expensive either. Our goal is to give you the highest quality repairs and service at the best possible price.

We do this by having Factory Trained Technicians to keep your vehicle safe. Our technicians train over 80 hours per year to know your vehicle better than anyone. Tthis ensures the highest performance of your vehicl We are the only shop in this market that represents exclusive Factory Parts to protect your investment.

Our Dealership Management System tracks and monitors your services and history to ensure that we take care of your vehicle to your standards and save you money throughout your ownership experience. We have pre-discounted menu prices to ensure you get the best possible price on repairs as well.

Does this sound like a great way to do business?

(D) Great! Let's get this important repair taken care of now!

The Dreaded Discount

Customers ask service advisors for a discount every day. When the professional service advisor discounts a service two things happen. The customer is trained that the price is not really the price and they can ask for a discount the next time. The other is that discounts diminish the value of the service. Many great retailers such as Apple Computers never provide a discount to their customers.

Customers perceive the value in the service and pay the retail price for the item. The dealership can have the same approach to its service By understanding that asking for a discount is simply the customer saying that they do not have enough information or perceive enough value to purchase at full price..

If the customer persists with the grind for a discount, it is important to remove part of that service. This is easy where there are multiple items requiring attention. The service advisor can perform three of the four items now at full price, and the customer can return later for the last service (at full price). When the service advisor "takes something away" it shows the intrinsic value of the product or service. This often refocuses the customer to the value of the dealership service.

Below are a few questions to ask the customer using the LEAD approach.

Can I get a discount?

- ✓ How much discount would you like?

- ✓ Why do you feel you need a discount?

- ✓ Do you have a budget for these repairs today?

- ✓ Would you like me to prioritize the repairs in order of importance

- ✓ Would you like to reschedule the work to accommodate your budget?

- ✓ Are you looking for the cheapest price or the best value?

- ✓ Has anyone ever told you how we price our work?

Asking for a discount is the customer's way of saying that there is not enough value in the items as they are described currently. This is another chance for the service advisor to use the dealership value statement.

Well, here at Hometown Motors, we believe in being competitive in the marketplace. We know that we are not the cheapest price for repairs, but we also know based on our research that we are not the most expensive either. Our goal is to give you the highest quality repairs and service at the best possible price.

We do this by having Factory Trained Technicians to keep your vehicle safe...Our technicians train over 80 hours per year to know your vehicle better than anyone. This ensures the highest performance of your vehicle...We are the only shop in this market that represents exclusive Factory Parts to protect your investment...

Our Dealership Management System tracks and monitors your services and history to ensure that we take care of your vehicle to your standards and save you money throughout your ownership experience...We have pre-discounted menu prices to ensure you get the best possible price on repairs as well.

Does this sound like a great way to do business?

A professional service advisor can begin to see the importance of the dealership value statement. This value statement is the professional service advisor's best weapon against discounting. Every time the customer talks price, the professional service advisor moves the conversation towards value to then build the value in the dealership. This is an amazing way for the professional service advisor to Master the Waiting Room.

The Service Department is constantly evolving and creates challenges daily. The Steve Shaw Training program has guided me as a Service Advisor with many of the service changes that occur with our customer trends. As a Service Manager, implementing processes from the program has helped groom our areas of the service department, resulting in increased revenue on what could have been missed opportunities."

Dwayne Granguillhome - Ford Truck Service Advisor

5

Advanced Objections Handling

Advanced Objections Handling - Questioning Approach - The 4 C's of Questioning

We ask questions to provoke thought and to gain insight into a customer's thought process. In selling, often the sales person is doing most of the talking. It is even more important to ask questions during the objection-handling phase. The service advisor must be able to ask these probing questions to get the proper result. Questioning can often be the hardest part of the sale. Some service advisors feel uncomfortable probing. Remember, that's where empathy comes in. Once the service advisor has established rapport with the customer, empathy and probing is a natural part of the sales process.

Service advisors can ask open-ended or close-ended questions. Open-ended questions allow the customer to speak their thoughts. An example of an open-ended question is "what is important to you for your service today?" The customer is forced to give a real answer about what is important to them. A close-ended question only requires a yes or no answer. An example would be "Is safety important to you?" The customer may say "No", and the service advisor is no further along in the conversation than before. It is important to ask open-ended questions to gain the insight needed.

Silence or Pause

Very often, after a question comes an awkward pause or silence from the customer. In advanced selling, it is important to become comfortable in the awkwardness. The customer is often formulating an answer to the question. WAIT; do not speak. A question was posed and now it's time for an answer from the customer. Let them speak next.

Four Types of questions

There are four types of questions the service advisor can ask the customer. They range from the simple rapport building to closing the sale. Questions will allow the service advisor to gain information.

Some questions build awareness, and other questions provoke the customer to realize the importance of the concern.

The four types of questions...

1. **Conditional** - These types of questions build rapport. They help you gain information.

2. **Concern** - These types of questions are asked to build awareness of the problem.

3. **Consequence** - These questions provoke the interviewee to realize the importance of the problem

4. **Close** - These types of questions help the customer to say yes to solving the problem

Conditional Questions - Rapport Building

1. How are you?
2. How do you like your car?
3. How do you drive your vehicle?
4. Do you tow a boat?
5. Do you travel in the mountains or desert?
6. What is important to you about maintaining your vehicle?
7. How long will you keep your vehicle?
8. Is this a lease or a purchase?

The point of these questions is to get the customer into rapport. The service advisor and the customer are having a conversation. The service advisor is hopefully learning valuable information about the customer. These questions are not just reserved for objection handling. These types of questions are asked during all aspects of the customer interaction process. However, many inexperienced sales people focus on the conditional question instead of probing further. Buyers quickly become bored if asked too many conditional questions. It is important to understand the different types of questions and how the service advisor can help move the sale forward. Asking questions provides a useful understanding and builds connection with the customer.

Concern Questions - Awareness

✓ Are you aware that transmission fluid, just like oil, requires service at regularly- scheduled intervals?

✓ Are you satisfied with the performance of your brake pads/tires?

✓ Has your vehicle given you the reliability you are looking for?

✓ Are you aware that by continuing to drive your vehicle the cost for future repairs could increase?

✓ Are you aware that the manufacturer has lease turn-in requirements

Concern questions build awareness of a problem for the customer. This helps create the need for the service or repair. The point of a concern question is to increase awareness and to build the case for the item that requires attention. Often sales people stop here. They introduce the problem and hope the customer will make the purchase. Sometimes awareness is enough, but it is important to take the next step and introduce consequences.

Consequence Questions - Consequences

✓ What happens if you _____

✓ Do you feel you will get the ... safety, performance, reliability, protection you are looking for by ignoring the concern?

✓ How much time will you spend looking for a second opinion?

✓ Just out of curiosity, how many times per year do you go the repair shop

Experienced sales people move quickly to the concequence. Asking more consequences questions often moves the customer to the solution on major sales. Consequence questions make the problem bigger. Making the problem larger is creating a larger need. If the need is great enough the sale becomes easier. Sometimes these questions are difficult to ask. Confidence will allow the professional service advisor the confidence to use the consequence question when the time is right. The point is learning how and when to use the tools in the service advisor's toolbox. Once the need is so great that the customer is ready to buy, then the service advisor can move in for the close.

Close Questions - Close

- ✓ If I could show you how to save money and get this item handled, would you be interested?
- ✓ Would you like to take care of this vital service now?

Professional sales people ask for the sale when the buyer is ready to purchase. Always ask for the sale.

Part 2

Transition to Real-World Selling

(Intentionally Left Blank)

Transition to Real-World Selling

The first part of this book presented the foundational selling approach. One could say selling is educating. If the customer is educated enough on the items presented, the only logical outcome is a sale. Another way to say it that selling is simply presenting material in a weighted fashion to derive an outcome. Selling fundamentals are needs and wants, features and benefits. It is important to understand that service advisors are selling needs to the customer. If a need is a requirement, then not making the repair will have consequences to the customer. The job of the service advisor is to find a way to present or educate the customer in a way to influence the customer to make a purchase. The earlier chapters have also provided tools to use in order to make the best presentation possible.

Often tools are pictured as mechanical equipment utilized by the shop technicians. The service advisor also has tools. The MPI approach is a tool for the service advisor to use at the appropriate time, just like the technician. The ABCs is another tool for the service advisor to use when selling. The LEAD approach to overcoming objections is another tool for the advisor's toolbox. In fact, all of the concepts presented in this book are tools to FILL the advisor's big bertha toolbox. Like an air gun, tools in the toolbox only work when they are in the hands of a capable technician. The air gun works much better when compressed air is hooked up as well.

Using the tools presented will only work when the service advisor pulls them out and speaks to the customer. Speaking with the power words is like compressed air spinning the lug nuts off the rims. It works! It works fast, and it is powerful!

The following chapters are designed to give real-world usage of the tools provided. They can be considered a "how-to" manual for applying the concepts. The best practice is for the service advisor to read and learn the concepts and either use what is presented, or, even better, create their own words to fit their own style. This will help the service advisor internalize the concepts and become fluent with the approaches presented.

6

The Either-Or-Close

Presenting Options

Customers are looking for options when servicing their vehicle. These options can be presented as two types of batteries, two or three types of tires, or the different options for a particular manufacturer part vs. an aftermarket part. Options help the customer make their best decision based on all the facts. The facts that the customer needs to know can be the variety of what is available. Other fact may be the price of the service down the street at the independent shop. Educating the customer on the variety of options creates a choice of multiple items instead of a yes or no choice. Provide the customer an option for a service, and the closing percentage goes from 50% for a yes- or-no question up to 66%-75%.

Another way to use options to the service advisor's advantage is to focus on the small difference in the price between the items. If the aftermarket price is $150 and the OEM is $200, the best approach is to sell the $50 difference. The service advisor can simply say that for only $50 more, the customer can have the best part for their car. As the service advisor builds a quote for the customer, it is important to research the competition to determine the prices elsewhere.

One great resource is to go to repairpal.com. Repairpal.com is a consumer website that provides the cost of most service items in the market. The customer can see the low to high price for nearly all service items. Use this website to ensure your cost is competitive, as well as to show the customer the cost down the street. This is a great way to present aftermarket alternatives to enhance the dealership's competitiveness.

As in any ABC presentation, it is most important to talk about the available options prior to presenting the cost. An ABC presentation for options is the same as an ABC presentation for one item, except for Customer Benefits. Typically the customer benefits are different based upon the warranty or the final type of service the customer chooses. Remember to present all the options first, then the cost, and finally the closing question.

To close the sale in presenting options, there is a variety of closing questions. Each one can be used to drive the customer to the best option the service advisor chooses. The first part of the question is ...

Which one of these...

The simple way to ask for the sale using the "Either - Or" Close is ...

Which one of these do you prefer?

If a customer is a price customer the service advisor can ask...

Which one of these options best fit your budget?

In some cases the service advisor may want to sell the higher priced option by asking...

Which one of these options best fits your lifestyle?

This close is especially effective with specialty vehicles such as Jeeps or Diesels. This can work with even Kia owners as the manufactures markets the Kia Lifestyle.

Pick the best option close for the situation. Remember to improve the sense of urgency the service advisor can add a power word to the close , such as:

Which one of these important services do you prefer now?

Many dealerships are implementing a strategy of using aftermarket parts to enhance the sales performance of the service department. This is arguably a great way to drive sales and RO Performance. Regardless of the tactic to use off-brand parts, presenting options IS a great way to improve sales.

Two years ago we began to implement the Steve Shaw Training Sales approach. My CSI, as well as my service department numbers have steadily grown. Steve makes it EASY to learn."

Brandon Santone – GM Service Advisor

7 Defection Points

A defection point is any time in the life cycle where the customer can "defect" from the dealership and go to an independent shop. Typically when the customer leaves the dealership for an independent shop they rarely return. The retention rate drops and everyone loses money.

The philosophy here is that value must overcome cost for any transaction to be successful. It is also appropriate to mention that the dealership must be competitive on certain items throughout the lifecycle. This pricing strategy is prevalent in all makes and models. The customer is judging the dealership at five key points as to their competitiveness in the market place. When the dealership demonstrates its competitive nature on these items, typically the customer believes that the other non-defection points are competitive as well. The customer is just more likely to return on the big-ticket items.

> A defection point is any time in the life cycle where the customer can "defect" the dealership and go to an independent repair shop.

There are five key defection points when a customer can leave the dealership.

The five Items to be priced competitively:

- ✓ LOF (Oil Change - Tire Rotation)
- ✓ Battery
- ✓ Brakes
- ✓ Tires
- ✓ Alignment

LOF - The LOF or Oil Change is the first time the customer is required to spend their money on maintenance. In fact, this is such a critical point that often the manufacturer or the dealership gives away the first one (or more) free. Some auto manufacturers give away two and three years of oil changes to tie the customer to the store. The dealership must price oil changes competitively to the market place. Often this is an opportunity to provide synthetic oil at regular prices or add additional value in the oil-change package. The customer must feel like they are getting a great price, or they will see the dealership as the high-price repair shop on the block and go elsewhere. They will defect because the perception is that anyone can perform an oil change.

Battery Replacement - The battery is another opportunity for the customer to defect from the dealership. Often the battery requires replacement at or around the end of the warranty period. Most customers know about the Sears Diehard Battery Special or the AutoZone Special. Customers believe anyone can replace a battery for a cheap price. The customer will leave the dealership over a high-priced battery. It is important to provide value and be competitive on the battery installation. An option is to give an amazing presentation and provide the customer with value and a competitive price. Many stores now offer free installation. Imagine a customer receiving a free battery as their vehicle approaches the end of a warranty or lease. This helps a customer see that the dealership cares about their wallet. This could even lead to more new car sales.

Brakes - The Brake replacement is a key defection point. Customers see advertisements for brakes on television and other advertising on a regular basis. Customers are aware that brakes are done at independent shops every day on every corner. It is vital for the dealership to remain competitive on brake repairs. The customer will shop brake prices. The dealership can offer the manufacturer value line (when available) and consider offering a quality aftermarket pad to the customer. This is true for highline stores as well as the others; customers feel that anyone is qualified to replace their brakes. A dealership that offers a competitive price on brakes will retain the customer through this volatile point in the life cycle.

Tires - Tires are actually the most dangerous point when most customers defect. Tire shops are on every corner, and most customers perceive that any mechanic can replace tires. Often dealership customers are not aware of the dealership participation in tire sales. Other times dealerships overcharge or overprice tires. Most dealerships that are in the tire sales arena understand that being in the service business means selling tires nearly at cost. Tires in these dealerships are sold at approximately 10% gross profit, and sometimes only $10 profit per tire. Another key point for tire sales is that tires are an impulse item for the customer. Dealership parts departments must stock a wide variety, or have right-now access to inventory. Dealers who do well with tires do well with maintenance and repairs. Dealers that perform well with maintenance perform well in their overall profit strategy. Therefore, tires are the key to the overall health of the vehicle maintenance and repair department.

Alignments - Alignments are required to protect the customer's investment in tires every year or 12,000 miles. This is a great time to show a customer that the dealership is competitive. Today alignments are becoming more and more complex, yet with the proper equipment, a maintenance alignment can be done in 30 minutes (often less) by the technician. It is important to keep technician flat rate hours to a minimum and sell alignments at a great price. Most competitive dealerships add a great incentive or spiff for the service advisor to offer alignments. This is a requirement at every 12,000 to 15,000 mile interval to protect the tire investment. Keep the price down to ensure the customer returns annually for this service.

Steve Shaw Training has been a great influence and his training program is leaps and bounds beyond any sales training I've had in the dealership environment."

Kenyon Pelkey – Kia – Fiat – Alfa Romeo Service Advisor

Scheduled Maintenance

Scheduled Maintenance vs. The LOF

Customer: "I am here today for an oil change"

Service Advisor: "Great! I have three options for you!"

This statement will make you money now. The next time a customer asks for an oil change, just say, "Great, I have three options for you!" Most service advisors have grown accustomed to saying OK to an oil change. Many have decided that the only thing that can be sold in the express or quick lane is a fast basic service. The truth is customers want options. Present the customer with options, and make some money.

The Basic Service - This is the **MINIMUM REQUIREMENT** from the manufacturer to maintain your warranty standards.

The Value Service - This is the best value. **MOST CUSTOMERS CHOOSE THIS ONE!**

The Premium Service - This is for customers who want to give their car the **BEST CARE!**

Ask the customer, "Which one do you prefer?"

No one actually knows what the customer will choose. However research shows that a customer with choices will choose something other than the basic service 50% of the time. Industry experts say customers choose the basic service 50% of the time, the value service 30% and the premium service 20%. This means that by making a presentation, the customer will choose more than an oil change, and the dealership and the service advisor can make money.

✓ Basic Service 50%   ✓ Value Service 30%   ✓ Premium Service 20%

Imagine a customer who owns a Mercedes Benz. Do they want to give their car the minimum requirement or possibly the *best care*?

Imagine a KIA owner. The KIA is a lifestyle. Do they want the minimum requirement or possibly the *best value* for their money?

Imagine a Corvette owner. Do these drivers want to maintain their vehicle to the minimum requirement, or do they want the best care?

Imagine any customer in the brand-specific dealership. Every service advisor has customers who only purchase the minimum. Others have some who want more. Often the customer who purchases the minimum does this because of the presentation (or lack of presentation.) What will the customer choose? The answer is unknown until the service advisor makes a presentation.

There are many ways to create a menu of services for the customer. It is important not to get caught up what is being presented. The important part here is the word path. Using the words "minimum requirements", "most customers choose", and "best care" are trigger words for the customer. They inspire a customer to make a decision about how they want to maintain their vehicle.

Basic Service = Minimum Requirements
Value Service = Most Customers Choose
Premium Service = Best Care

The customer will choose one of the options if presented. If the service advisor chooses to only take an order for an oil change, it is certainly guaranteed that an oil change will be performed.

With Steve Shaw's training and easy to remember word tracks, I went from being a brand new advisor to the LEAD advisor on the service drive. His easy tips and tricks turned my job into a career."

Matt Maynard – Kia Service Advisor

Here is a simple proposed way to have options for the customer.

Basic Service = Minimum Requirements

- ✓ Oil Change
- ✓ Tire Rotation
- ✓ MPI

Value Service = Most Customers Choose

- ✓ Oil Change
- ✓ Tire Rotation
- ✓ MPI
- ✓ Wiper Blades
- ✓ Tire Balance
- ✓ Air Filter
- ✓ Cabin Filter

Premium Service = Best Care

- ✓ Oil Change
- ✓ Tire Rotation
- ✓ Tire Balance
- ✓ MPI
- ✓ Air Filter
- ✓ Cabin Filter
- ✓ Wiper Blades
- ✓ Fuel Induction
- ✓ Alignment

Imagine any brand of vehicle and their customers. Many dealerships and manufacturers offer free first oil changes. This is for retention purposes. When does the customer love their car the most? Correct: when they buy the vehicle. The first oil change is the time to talk about options. This is the time when the customer is most likely to buy the premium service. Certainly the dealership can deduct the cost of the free oil change from the premium service. This is the time to get the customer used to more than an oil change.

Menu Selling vs Quarter Time

Service Advisors are confronted with the pressure of Quarter Time every day. Many dealerships struggle for a number of reasons not to make the actual 15-minute window for MPI sales presentations. Presenting scheduled maintenance is an amazing solution for this pressure. When the service advisor sells more service in the drive, the total time for service completion is lengthened. This adds to the time for Quarter time. Quarter time becomes 30 minutes or more. The more items sold, the longer the time. The longer the time, the less pressure on everyone to complete the process. This also ensures that the Repair Order Performance is improving. And this lessens the actual need for an MPI. The items that require attention based on time and mileage are sold.

Quarter Time vs Menu Selling

Below is a table with the estimated times and Quarter time equivalent.

Estimated Time to Complete	Service Required	Estimated Quarter Time in Minutes
60 Minutes	**Basic Service** • Oil Change • Tire Rotation • MPI	15 Minutes *High Pressure for MPI Completion*
120 Minutes	**Value Service** • Oil Change • Tire Rotation • MPI • Air Filter • Cabin Filter • Wiper Blades • Tire Balance	30 Minutes *Medium Pressure for MPI Completion*
240 Minutes	**Premium Service** • Oil Change • Tire Rotation • Tire Balance • MPI • Air Filter • Cabin Filter • Wiper Blades • Tire Balance • Fuel Induction • Alignment	60 Minutes *Low Pressure for MPI Completion*

Hours Per RO with Menu Selling

This next table is the estimated Flat Rate Hours FRH paid to the technician, which determines a service advisor's repair order performance in HOURS / RO.

Service Required	Estimated FRH Paid or Hours Per RO
Basic Service • Oil Change • Tire Rotation • MPI	.3 .3 *Total FRH .6*
Value Service • Oil Change • Tire Rotation • MPI • Air Filter • Cabin Filter • Wiper Blades • Tire Balance	.3 .3 .3 .3 .1 .5 *Total FRH 1.6*
Premium Service • Oil Change • Tire Rotation • Tire Balance • MPI • Air Filter • Cabin Filter • Wiper Blades • Tire Balance • Fuel Induction • Alignment	.3 .3 .3 .3 .1 .5 1.0 1.0 *Total FRH 3.6*

The above table proves that the service advisor has up to 3.6 FRH to sell on every service over 10,000 miles. This can and will improve repair order performance. The days of only selling an oil change are over. A simple oil change is .6 FRH. A value service is 1.6 FRH. A premium service is 3.6 FRH.

This type of scheduled maintenance can be performed on any vehicle over one year and approximately 10,000 miles. The key is in the word path. The service advisor is not requiring the customer to make a purchase. The service advisor is simply presenting options to the customer that the dealership provides. In the old days, the service advisor would talk about manufacturer requirements and dealer-recommended services. Remember, the customer does not want recommendations. Customers want options. This is simply making a menu for the customer to choose from. The customer will select the level of service that they want to maintain their vehicle.

Selling scheduled maintenance in the service drive is a key to repair order performance. The professional service advisor sells scheduled maintenance over oil changes. The professional service advisor presents options to the customer. Most importantly, every time the customer comes in for service seeking an oil change, the service advisor responds with..."Great! I have (two or) three options"... Practice over and over. Watch the repair order performance improve, and notice the additional money in your paycheck. Certainly the dealership can create a "good, better, best" scenario for all of these services. Present the customer with menu options. It is proven that customers will chose more than just an oil change, the minimum standard. Master the Waiting Room, and sell service at scheduled maintenance intervals.

9 Fluid Maintenance

Dealerships and service advisors who participate in a fluid maintenance program typically have a higher repair order performance. Over the years there have been many discussions about the validity and need for additional fluid maintenance. Similar to scheduled maintenance, many customers want more for their vehicle. The job of the service advisor is to present the variety of services that are offered by the dealership. The service advisor is not required to make a decision on the validity of the service. The service advisor is required to present options for the customer. Studies show that a dealership with a fluid maintenance program is likely to have up to 1.0 hours more per repair order than a dealership that does not have a professional program. It is important for service advisors to understand the basics of fluid and its purpose in a vehicle's maintenance and lubrication system.

The fluids used throughout an automobile's various systems serve many purposes, such as lubrication, heat transfer, hydraulics and suspension of contaminants. There are many systems in an automobile that rely on having clean fluid of the proper specification in order to function properly, such as the engine, transmission, power steering, cooling and brake system. Over time and as a result of normal use, these fluids become contaminated and/or break down until they reach a point at which they are no longer able to provide the protection or properly perform the functions for which they were intended. When this occurs, it can result in diminished performance, premature wear, and/or damage to components within the affected system.

Fluid exchange services performed at regular intervals ensure that the systems these fluids protect operate at peak performance. This helps keep the vehicle dependable, keeps passengers safe, and saves time and money by preventing compromised performance or system failure brought on by the premature wear of system components.

Nothing is more important than clean fluid and filterization to properly maintain any vehicle. I have seen hundreds of service advisors use Steve Shaw Training word tracks to improve their fluid maintenance sales and increase their paychecks."
James Gross – BG Products Fluid Maintenance Consultant

The following pages contain the required information and additional tools needed to make the best fluid maintenance presentations to the customer. An ABC presentation with the word path is included for most fluid maintenance services that are sold in the dealership. This will help all levels of the professional service advisor improve their RO performance.

Fuel Injector Cleaner

The Fuel Injector cleaner is a premium, low-odor detergent compound for professional fuel rail and injector cleaning using an injection tool. This service restores engine power lost due to dirty injectors and fouled combustion chambers.

Talking Points

- ✓ Cleans fuel injectors of deposits
- ✓ Cleans combustion chamber
- ✓ Improves engine performance loss due to dirty injectors
- ✓ Contains NO alcohol
- ✓ Contains PEA Technology
- ✓ Has no environmentally harmful dyes

Benefits

- ✓ Extends Life of Fuel System Components - Protects Investment
- ✓ Maintains Fuel Economy - Protects Investment (Saves Money)
- ✓ Keeps Vehicle Reliable and Dependable
- ✓ Ensures Vehicle Safety on the Road

ABC Presentation for Fuel Injector Cleaner

The item that requires attention today is your fuel system.

The reason it needs service is based on time and mileage. It is important to clean your injectors every 15,000 miles or nnn months.

The benefits to you are to help extend the life of the injector system, maintain optimal fuel economy and ensure your vehicle is reliable and dependable.

The way we do this here at our dealership is to hook a performance tool into the fuel rail and clean the injectors at the source.

The total cost is only XX.XX.

May I have your permission to take care of this important service now?

Fuel System Cleaner

The Fuel System Cleaner is a fast-acting blend of cleaners and detergents that you pour right into the gas tank to boost performance and gas mileage. It removes deposits in combustion chambers, intake manifolds, ports, and valves and restores flow in fuel injectors.

Talking Points

✓ Restores engine performance loss due to dirty fuel system

✓ Improves fuel combustion, keeping fuel system clean

✓ Cleans fuel injectors and carburetors

✓ Contains NO alcohol

✓ Contains PEA Technology

✓ Has no environmentally harmful dyes

Benefits

✓ Extends Life of Fuel System Components - Protects Investment

✓ Maintains Fuel Economy - Protects Investment (Saves Money)

✓ Keeps Vehicle Reliable and Dependable

✓ Ensures Vehicle Safety on the Road

ABC Presentation for Fuel System Cleaner

The item that requires attention today is your fuel system.

The reason it needs service is based on time and mileage. It is important to clean your fuel system every 15,000 miles.

The benefits to you are to help extend the life of the fuel system, maintain optimal fuel economy and ensure your vehicle is reliable and dependable.

The way we do this here at our dealership is to simply pour our exclusive cleaner into the fuel tank.

The total cost is only XX.XX.

May I have your permission to take care of this important service now?

Cooling System - Fluid Exchange

The Cooling System Fluid Exchange removes built-up scale and harsh mineral deposits that have formed in the cooling system. It removes tough residues caused by coolant inhibitor breakdown.

Talking Points

- ✓ Removes scale deposits
- ✓ Cleans heat transfer surfaces
- ✓ Helps promote more efficient heat transfer
- ✓ Helps improve coolant circulation
- ✓ Is compatible with most types of antifreeze
- ✓ Has no environmentally harmful dyes

Benefits

- ✓ Extends life of Cooling System and Components - Protects Investment (Saves Money)
- ✓ Extends Life of Transmission System - Protects Investment (SavEs Money)
- ✓ Ensures Better Cooling System Performance
- ✓ Saves time and Money on Preventable Repairs - Protects Investment
- ✓ Keeps Vehicle Reliable and Dependable
- ✓ Ensures Vehicle Safety on the Road

ABC Presentation for Coolant Fluid Exchange

The item that requires attention today is your cooling system.

The reason it needs to be serviced is that it is required based on time and mileage. It is important to service your cooling system every 30,000 miles.

The benefits to you are to extend the life of the cooling system and components. It also keeps the transmission fluid cool as well. This will protect your investment and save money on future repairs.

The total cost today is only XX.XX.

May I have your permission to take care of this vital service now?

Engine Treatment

The Engine Treatment is a combination of lubricants and performance-enhancing metal conditioners to boost lubrication protection. It helps reduce engine oil oxidation and thickening under intense driving conditions, such as trailering or hauling heavy loads.

Talking Points

- ✓ Improves oil viscosity & Boosts engine lubrication
- ✓ Helps safely remove sludge and varnish buildup
- ✓ Reduces engine friction and wear
- ✓ Provides extra protection for heavily loaded engines
- ✓ Protects against bearing corrosion
- ✓ Fortifies against oxidation and thermal breakdown
- ✓ Is compatible with all types of motor oils
- ✓ Contains No environmentally harmful dyes

Benefits

- ✓ Extends Life of Engine Components - Protects Investment
- ✓ Maintains Fuel Economy - Saves Money
- ✓ Keeps Vehicle Reliable and Dependable
- ✓ Ensures Vehicle Safety on the Road

ABC Presentation for Engine Treatment

The item that requires attention today is your engine maintenance.

The reason it needs service is based on time and mileage.

The benefits to you are to help extend the life of the engine, maintain fuel economy and ensure your vehicle is safe on the road.

The total cost today is only $XX.XX.

May I have your permission to take care of this important service now?

Intake and Combustion Chamber Flush

The Intake and Combustion Chamber Flush is designed to be introduced into the induction system with a special vacuum or high-pressure fogger tool. It cleans and removes varnish and carbon build-up in the intake and induction system.

Talking Points

✓ Removes intake manifold/valve deposits

✓ Removes combustion chamber deposits

✓ Improves proper fuel/air mixture and engine performance

✓ Improves engine performance

✓ Contains NO alcohol and No environmentally harmful dyes

✓ Contains PEA Technology

Benefits

✓ Extends Life of Fuel System Components - Protects Investment

✓ Maintains Fuel Economy - Protects Investment (Saves Money)

✓ Keeps Vehicle Reliable and Dependable

✓ Ensures Vehicle Safety on the Road

ABC Presentation for Intake and Combustion Chamber Flush

The item that requires attention today is your fuel system.

The reason it needs service is based on time and mileage. It is important to clean your injectors every 15,000 miles.

The benefits to you are to help extend the life of the injector system, maintain optimal fuel economy and ensure your vehicle is reliable and dependable.

The way we do this here at our dealership is to hook up a performance tool to the Intake and fuel system with a special vacuum or high-pressure fogger tool.

The total cost is only XX.XX.

May I have your permission to take care of this important service now?

Power Steering System - Fluid Exchange

The Power Steering Treatment contains anti-oxidants, dispersants, and powerful metal conditioners to improve the power steering fluid's oxidation resistance, lubrication properties, and ability to withstand heat. It also helps reduce deposits.

Talking Points

✓ Provides extra lubrication to power steering

✓ Helps reduce steering pump noise and resist fluid oxidation

✓ Provides extra corrosion protection

✓ Helps power steering system run cleaner

✓ Is compatible with all types of fluids

✓ Contains no environmentally harmful dyes

Benefits

✓ Extends life of Power Steering System and Components - Protects Investment (Saves Money)

✓ Ensures Better Power Steering System Performance

✓ Saves time and Money on Preventable Repairs - Protects Investment

✓ Keeps Vehicle Reliable and Dependable

✓ Ensure Vehicle Safety on the Road

ABC Presentation for Power Steering Fluid Exchange

The item that requires attention today is your power steering system.

The reason it needs to be serviced is that it is required based on time and mileage. It is important to service your power steering system every 30,000 miles.

The benefits to you are to extend the life of the power steering system and components. This will protect your investment and save money on future repairs.

The way we do this is to use a performance tool to extract and replace old fluid with new fluid. Once this is completed we will add a conditioner to supplement the new fluid to clean and enhance the performance of the system.

The total cost today is only XX.XX.

May I have your permission to take care of this vital service now?

Brake Fluid System - Fluid Exchange

The Brake Fluid Exchange provides the ultimate high temperature, moisture resistant lubrication.

Talking Points

- ✓ Dot 3 and Dot 4 Protections
- ✓ High Temperature Standards

Benefits

- ✓ Extends life of Brake System and Components - Protects Investment (Saves Money)
- ✓ Ensures Better Brake System Performance
- ✓ Saves time and Money on Preventable Repairs - Protecst Investment
- ✓ Keeps Vehicle Reliable and Dependable
- ✓ Ensures Vehicle Safety on the Road

ABC Presentation for Brake Fluid Exchange

The item that requires attention today is your brake fluid system.

The reason it needs to be serviced is that it is required based on time and mileage. It is important to service your brake system every 30,000 miles.

The benefits to you are to extend the life of the brake system and components. This will protect your investment and save money on future repairs.

The way we do this is to hook up a brake performance tool to pressure bleed the brake system. While bleeding old fluid, new fluid pushes the old contaminated fluid through the system and out, restoring the brake fluid to a like-new condition, thus giving you that hard pedal you are accustomed to having.

The total cost today is only XX.XX.

May I have your permission to take care of this vital service now?

Transmission System - Fluid Exchange

The Transmission Fluid Cleaner is a special additive to provide extra lubrication protection to automatic transmissions. It is added to new and remaining transmission fluid left behind in the torque converter after a drain and refill service. It helps prevent deposit formation and fluid breakdown. It also helps prevent transmission shudder and shifting problems and prevents transmission leaks by keeping seals soft and pliable.

Talking Points

- ✓ Helps reduce wear
- ✓ Helps keep transmission clean
- ✓ Resists fluid oxidation and deposits
- ✓ Conditions seals and O-Rings
- ✓ Helps maintain proper viscosity
- ✓ Helps prevent oxidation and acid formation
- ✓ Replaces essential additives in ATF

Benefits

- ✓ Extends life of Transmission System and Components - Protects Investment (Saves Money)
- ✓ Ensures Better Transmission System Performance
- ✓ Saves time and Money on Preventable Repairs - Protects Investment
- ✓ Keeps Vehicle Reliable and Dependable
- ✓ Ensures Vehicle Safety on the Road

ABC Presentation for Transmission Fluid Exchange

The item that requires attention today is your transmission system.

The reason it needs to be serviced is that it is required based on time and mileage. It is important to service your transmission system every 30,000 miles.

The benefits to you are to extend the life of the transmission system and components. It also keeps the transmission fluid cool. This will protect your investment and save money on future repairs.

The total cost today is only XX.XX.

May I have your permission to take care of this vital service now?

10 Customer Satisfaction Index (CSI) and my Paycheck

People who can sell are typically in command in a dealership. They are held in high regard, because selling is what the business is all about. Often high-performance sales people are given some latitude when it comes to CSI scores. Service advisors who have high CSI and truly take care of their customers are also given similar latitude. The real deal Master Of the Waiting Room service advisor can do both sales and CSI. They can and do both extremely well.

Most customers want to get their needs addressed. Their needs are safety, performance, reliability and protection of their investment. Once this is handled, the customer is most likely to give the service advisor the best score possible. The key points of getting a great score are to actually give great service and to educate the customer on the process. Most manufacturers frown on coaching for the score. The reality is the more educated the customer, the better the score.

At the conclusion of the writeup process, the service advisor can simply tell the customer that today is going to be the best day for service. Advise the customer that they are going to get the best service that they have ever had. Smile. Shake their hand good bye. Live up to the commitments made during the write up. Call the customer at the established promised times. After the MPI presentation, feel free to talk about CSI. Do the best job of informing the customer of their needs and status. Towards the end of the delivery process, simply ask the customer if they had great service today. If so... please let the manufacturer know you were given excellent service.

ASK for the score you deserve. Too many advisors only say "take care of me". Here is the best word path and approach.

At Write Up

It is going to be my pleasure to give you excellent service today

At MPI

Has your service been excellent so far?

At Delivery

Was your service excellent today? Great! It is always my pleasure to take care of you and your car. An even great pleasure for me would be to hear you tell the manufacturer you received "excellent service":

- ✓ By scoring us with all 10's
- ✓ By scoring us with all 100's
- ✓ By telling them you LOVE the dealership
- ✓ By scoring us with *"Your Words"*

Regardless of the dealership or manufacturer, planting the seed is important. Everyone wants their service and their performance to stand on its own. In today's world an educated consumer is the best consumer. Today's world is full of email and text messages. Certainly utilize these technologies for the highest benefit. Standing in front of a customer and committing to the best performance will deliver the best results. When a service advisor delivers on the performance and educates the consumer on the process, it will serve the service advisor well.

The "Pleasure Pleasure" CSI Letter

When using digital media (or even snail mail) to communicate with a customer, a great approach to influencing the customer is called the "Pleasure Pleasure" principle. By using the word "pleasure" in a conversation twice, it opens the customer's mind to what specific words come in quotation marks after the second time the word "Pleasure" appears. Often the customer will repeat exactly what is in the quotation marks.

The training that Steve gave myself when building our Customer Retention Department was a game changer. The return of our Customer Service Surveys went up over 300%. We also increased our CSE score from dead last to the top 5 percent in Honda in the nation. Steve Shaw Training word tracks were instrumental for the success we have had in our customer service and retention department."

Brendan Rizza – CSI

Example

It was my pleasure to service your vehicle recently. An even greater pleasure would be to hear you say to the manufacturer that you received "excellent service".

- ✓ That you love your dealership
- ✓ That you received truly exceptional service
- ✓ That you received excellent service by scoring us with all 10s
- ✓ That you received excellent service by scoring us with all 100s

Setting the Next Appointment

Management is working with marketing companies, search engines, mailers, door hangers and almost any other method imaginable to create and retain customers. Setting the next appointment is the highest-impact item a service advisor can do to ensure their personal long-term success at the dealership. The service advisor just gained a commitment from the customer to tell the manufacturer that they love the dealership and the service they just received are now happily involved with the dealership. This is the time to strike and ask to set the next appointment. That appointment can be based on any given scenario of maintenance. This scenario can be 90 Days, six months or one year. Set the appointment. This puts the customer in the frame of mind to return to the dealership and commit to the service advisor. The service advisor is building repeat business and long term loyalty.

Over the next period of time, the service advisor can be working with established customers who they know and who want to have service with them exclusively. This is a dream scenario for the professional service advisor. Customers will BUY from those they **LIKE** and **TRUST**. Create this process for personal success in the dealership.

Example:

I have you scheduled with ME for your next maintenance service on XXX date. The dealership will confirm with you a few days ahead to make sure this still works for you. It is my pleasure to serve you and your family.

11 Summary

This entire book is designed to be a position manual for the professional service advisor. The book began by examining the desires of the customer. The customer is looking for safety, performance, reliability and protecting their investment. Every time a service advisor opens their mouth to sell anything to a customer, one or more of those trigger words must come out! This will make selling easier. Customers will make a purchase if the service advisor offers them what they want, not what they do not want. Customers do want safety, not tires. They want performance, not an air conditioning compressor. Customers want reliability, not brake pads. They want to protect their investment. Use these powerful words to make more money.

The MPI is the most valuable tool in the service advisor's toolbox. Customers want to know everything about their car. They do not want to know what is wrong. Always ask permission to present the information. Use the word tracks from the book. 1)Call the customer by their name. 2) Make sure the customer knows the Year, Make, Model, and Mileage of their vehicle. 3) Start at the top and work down the inspection report. Use the words PASS/FAIL when presenting items. Customers want to hear the facts about their car, not opinions (such as great, good, perfect).

The item PASSES our vehicle inspection.
The item FAILS our vehicle inspection.

Conclude the inspection with the simple close.

I know this is a lot of information; do you have any questions for me about the health of your car?

Propose to provide a quote for the failed items. Present the quote the way the customer wants it provided: either present a grand total, RIM or line-by-line. The way the customer requested to be SOLD!

Learn, utilize and internalize the ABCs of selling. Every sale is exactly the same. The sale starts with A and ends with the CLOSE.

The item that requires attention today is ____. The reason it needs to be replaced is ____. The benefits to you are 1) ____ 2) ____ 3) ____. The way

*we do this at our dealership is _____ . **The total investment is $ ____. May I have your permission to perform this vital service now?***

This word path will keep the professional service advisor on track. The service advisor can expand or contract the presentation based on the style of the customer.

Internalize the LEAD approach to overcoming objections. Listen and restate the customer's objections. Be sure to acknowledge the customer's objection. Show empathy. Align with the customer to demonstrate caring. Ask clarifying questions to discover the root cause of the objection, and lead the customer as a partner to solving their dilemma. Determine the most appropriate solution for the customer.

Asking questions is a learned skill. Become the master of questions. This is the key to understanding the customer's needs and wants. Once the service advisor masters questions, the world opens up. The four types of questions are: 1) Conditional 2) Concern, 3) Consequence 4) Close.

Alignments can be presented to every customer over 12,000 miles to protect their investment. Fluid Maintenance can drive sales up an additional hour per RO or more.

The professional service advisor now has a scripted presentation for each fluid maintenance product. When the customer is presented the maintenance requirements to maintain their car, customers will be happy to purchase what they desire for their vehicle..

Keep an eye out for the defection points. Work with service management to ensure the five key components are priced competitively.

- ✓ LOF
- ✓ Battery
- ✓ Tires
- ✓ Alignment
- ✓ Brakes

These items are the key to retention. Never let a customer leave the dealership over price/value on a defection point. They rarely return for a future visit.

Consider the three types of menu services that the dealership can provide: basic, value and premium. No one knows what any customer will purchase until the presentation is given.

" Steve Shaw Training has helped me improve my performance and paycheck as a service advisor and manager."

Stacy Dalphonse – Nissan Service Advisor

(Intentionally Left Blank)

Send Off

Bob Cawley
Director of Fixed Operations
Horne Auto Group

....

The only thing better than reading this book is ... putting it into action.

Service Advisors always wonder if this stuff works in the real world. Service Advisors seem to question the practical application of training. Master of the Waiting Room principles WORK. Service Advisors who practice the selling approach spelled out in this book **MAKE MORE MONEY!**

I would like to share a story about Michael, a Hyundai Service Advisor. Michael was an average performer. He also was a little hard headed and felt like he already had the process down. Enter Steve Shaw and *"The Master of the Waiting Room"*. Michael listened, implemented, practiced and methodically perfected his presentation. The principles in this book were brought to life through continued practice. He used the power words to prevent objections and express the need for action. He learned how to use empathy to overcome objections.

The results showed up in his Key Performance Indicators and his paycheck. Michael averages 2.1 hours per customer pay repair order. This young man earned nearly $100,000 last year. He will certainly top this going forward! Did I mention that he is doing this at a Hyundai Store? I enjoy standing close by and listening to him speak with his customers. He uses the same system every time and it works. Our Dealer Principle wants him talking to customers. *He is a Master of the Waiting Room.*

Congratulations for reading this book. Keep it in a handy spot. Continue to study the principles of this book. I can assure you this, if you take these secrets to heart and apply them to your daily work ethic, you will become a more successful service advisor and provide for yourself and your family as never before. You too will become *Master of the Waiting Room!*

(Intentionally Left Blank)

Parting words from Steve

The profession of being a service advisor is honorable. A service advisor is a career position to inspire towards and achieve greatness. A service advisor is a skilled practitioner of many disciplines. This job requires the ability to interact and communicate with the public. This job requires the professional service advisor to understand the numerous warranties and warranty systems. This includes the current year and all the years with sometimes-radical changes to vehicle and regulatory compliance. This job of a professional service advisor, on top of everything else, is sales and Customer Retention Focused.

Men, women, families and the young and old rely on a highly trained service advisor to guide them through their automotive trials. Most people are unaware about the complexity of this job. The veteran service advisor practices all of these skills with ease and with little recognition. The service advisor gains satisfaction by solving problems the right way. The job itself is the satisfaction. Most go day to day with the light in their heart to make others day a little bit better. These talents, combined with the skills presented in this book, transform the Professional Service Advisor into a *Master of the Waiting Room*.

The Master of the Waiting Room provides their dealership tremendous profit, more so than most new car sales persons. The Master of the Waiting room knows and works for customer retention. The Master of the Waiting Room earns healthy living and provides for their family. The Master of the Waiting Room practices the craft and practices the art of selling. The Master of the Waiting Room is a passionate servant of the dealership. The Master of the Waiting Room willingly serves to improve the lives of the entire dealership team. This Master is the one who the Dealer Principal wants in the Waiting Room with the Service Customer - Selling - Retaining - Being!

Congratulations on your future victory. You are the Master of the Waiting Room!

Steve Shaw

Testimonials

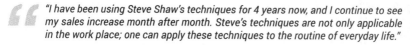

"I have been using Steve Shaw's techniques for 4 years now, and I continue to see my sales increase month after month. Steve's techniques are not only applicable in the work place; one can apply these techniques to the routine of everyday life."

Corey Smith – Toyota Service Advisor

"Steve Shaw Training approach taught me how to improve my performance by sharing the value to my customers. Steve's in depth method to explaining the vehicle health report allowed me to explain the vehicle's maintenance needs to the customer in a way that they felt the importance of the service."

Grace Hardin – Ford Service Advisor

"As a 21-year veteran service advisor, it is great to go back to the basics for success. Creating a need for the customer is vital to the sale. The ABCs are the foundation to make more money. I always pick up new information in every class. Steve Shaw Training always gets our team focused on selling."

Brooks Falzone – Honda Service Advisor

"Steve Shaw Training shows you how to accept customers properly, listen to them, and helps you understand their needs so that they feel comfortable when coming into your dealership! The approach helps customers buy more service."

Richard Anderson – Jaguar Service Advisor

The Service Department is constantly evolving and creates challenges daily. The Steve Shaw Training program has guided me as a Service Advisor with many of the service changes that occur with our customer trends. As a Service Manager, implementing processes from the program has helped groom our areas of the service department, resulting in increased revenue on what could have been missed opportunities.""

Dwayne Granguillhome - Ford Truck Service Advisor

"Steve Shaw Training approach gave me the skills and knowledge of dealing with customers who need to repair their cars but were hesitant to spend money at the dealership. Now I have the confidence of helping the client make the right buying decisions."

Armen Mansouri - Porsche Service Advisor

Steve Shaw provides a fresh new approach to increasing sales in the service drive. His real life automotive experiences and up-to-date practices drive results. Steve Shaw's training is impressive, and highly effective."

Stephanie Wilson – Corporate Service Drive Trainer

Two years ago we began to implement the Steve Shaw Training Sales approach. My CSI, as well as my service department numbers have steadily grown. Steve makes it EASY to learn."

Brandon Santone – GM Service Advisor

"Steve Shaw Training has been a great influence and his training program is leaps and bounds beyond any sales training I've had in the dealership environment."

Kenyon Pelkey – Kia – Fiat – Alfa Romeo Service Advisor

"With Steve Shaw's training and easy to remember word tracks, I went from being a brand new advisor to the LEAD advisor on the service drive. His easy tips and tricks turned my job into a career."

Matt Maynard – Kia Service Advisor

"Nothing is more important than clean fluid and filterization to properly maintain any vehicle. I have seen hundreds of service advisors use Steve Shaw Training word tracks to improve their fluid maintenance sales and increase their paychecks."

James Gross – BG Products Fluid Maintenance Consultant

"The training that Steve gave myself when building our Customer Retention Department was a game changer. The return of our Customer Service Surveys went up over 300%. We also increased our CSE score from dead last to the top 5 percent in Honda in the nation. Steve Shaw Training word tracks were instrumental for the success we have had in our customer service and retention department."

Brendan Rizza – CSI

"Steve Shaw Training has helped me improve my performance and paycheck as a service advisor and manager."

Stacy Dalphonse – Nissan Service Advisor

Notes

Notes

Notes

Notes

Notes

Notes